This Interim Time

This Interim Time

Essays

Oona Frawley

THE LILLIPUT PRESS
DUBLIN

First published 2025 by
THE LILLIPUT PRESS
62–63 Sitric Road,
Arbour Hill,
Dublin 7,
Ireland
www.lilliputpress.ie

10 9 8 7 6 5 4 3 2 1

A CIP record for this title is available from The British Library.

Paperback ISBN 978 1 84351 922 5
eBook ISBN 978 1 84351 940 9

Lilliput gratefully acknowledges the financial support of the Arts Council / An Chomhairle Ealaíon.

Set in 12 pt on 16 pt Adobe Caslon Pro and BB Modern Pro by Compuscript
Printed and bound in Ireland by Sprint Books

For my parents, and in memory
of Nancy Falkow McBride

HOUSES

For years I tried to write a novel that began with the consequences of my parents' emigration from Ireland to the US. I amassed pages and pages and never found a way of putting it down, because I didn't want to say what had led to their departure so many years before I was born. It seemed hard and unforgiving, to expose my father in that way, to examine my mother's mortification so long after the fact. But after I'd made the reverse migration and settled in Ireland as an adult, I thought about what had led them to leave. I wrote the opening pages of the novel in sight of the sea in Mayo, at dusk on a warm summer's evening, in a beach house belonging to my husband's family. My baby and young child were finally asleep, my husband was working and would join us at the weekend. While the room was suffused with pinkening light, I wrote until it was almost too dark to see and the baby woke up, crying for me.

*

I wrote at the dining room table under a large window that faced the sea. Initially I wrote about a metal stage make-up box that lived in a closet in my childhood apartment. Its image appeared to me quite suddenly the first evening: the dark green sheen of the paint, the clasp speckled with minute grains of rust. The box was cantilevered, opening smoothly and expanding like a tiered theatre in a way that enthralled me as a small child. Unfolding, it released the tickling odour of powder, the heavier note of Max Factor pastes Peach Special, and Peach Dark in mustard-yellow metal tubes. There was Pan-Stik in Natural and Fair, the twisting mechanism at their bases sticky from make-up application through the years. Several tins of Pan-Cake had been cratered by sponges; one tint was ghostly, its sponge stiff and lacy white. The top layer of the make-up box contained what appeared fat, sticky crayons wrapped in gold paper: lip, cheek and eye colour, but also the colour for bruises, shadowing, abrasions, cuts. There were small collections of brushes and sponges in a middle tier and in the bottom an array of hair pieces that could be attached with combs and bobby pins in different sizes that clattered through my fingers. It was a box for transformation, but also a way of seeing into my parents' pasts. I saw it before me on the table in Mayo, imagined undoing the clasp and unfolding the box to peer into it. I pictured my parents sitting in the dressing rooms of different theatres with the box's contents strewn before them, applying their make-up before mirrors ringed by bare bulbs, in preparation for evening performances.

*

As a child surrounded by stage actors, I grew up in a space in which failure was a part of day-to-day life. Before an audition, my father might talk to his agent, rehearse with me, meet other actors for a run-through, go to the actual event. The follow-up involved chats with friends, discussion with my mother and me. If a congratulatory call came from his agent that evening, he'd cleared a hurdle. Success had been achieved.

Of course, in a place like New York City where not just waitstaff but doormen, taxi drivers, hairdressers, teachers, lawyers and brokers had stage dreams, he was not always successful – not even mostly successful. He and his friends discussed bombed auditions so often and with such relishing of detail that when I was seven I decided that the theatre was not for me. So when at a dinner party not long afterwards I was asked confidentially by a doorman-actor friend of my parents if I too would become an actor when I grew up, I shook my head and told him that I wanted a more stable career. What would that be? he asked me. There were guffaws and much hilarity when I told them that I would be a writer.

Auditions sounded like harrowing experiences. Pretend to be someone else – briefly – and if you were convincing enough you were cast as that person. I could see, even at that age, that there was great satisfaction to be gained by having someone give you the part. But what I didn't realise until I was slightly older was that success did not arrive with the awarding of the part, which was only the beginning of another set of failures. There was – a lightbulb moment for me about this phrase as a child – no resting on one's laurels. That coinage wasn't an admonition to the lazy, just a reflection of day-to-day realities: any success, whatever that looked like, was temporary. You got the part, but then rehearsals began. Some days were terrible: so terrible that you left doubting your ability to inhabit the role after all; you knew the understudy, usually playing another, smaller role, was eying you and limbering up your speeches in their mind. Other days were better, and you thought you could do it: there were moments when the self disappeared and you were flooded by the strange exhilaration of another person coming to life through you. Then previews began and the cycle of terrible and better began again. Even during 'successful' runs, when reviews were good and audiences streamed in through heavy doors, there were nights when strange things happened – when laughter died, or lines were swallowed, or a mood took the theatre like a hostage – and it all felt terribly wrong. There was no consistent success, no point at which one could say: the show – or, more personally – *I* have been a success. Failure was a part of the project at all times.

*

I do not know as I write in Mayo that the novel will fail. I know only that, for the first time since the birth of my second child, a chink of time opens up and in it I will begin a project that will take up the corners of my life for over ten years.

*

It is my first time in this house by the sea in Mayo in the west of Ireland. The children and I drove across the country from our home in Wicklow, the car full of pillows and duvets, buckets and spades, beloved teddies, breaking the journey in Strokestown so that they could empty their legs of some of the eagerness to arrive. I had seen photos of the house I am staying in, heard stories about my husband's family visits here. No pictures have done it justice, and the stories, now that I am here, seem as if they were about somewhere else. Those tales were mostly about rain, often about mist and the heaviness of wet sand at the beach. But I am gazing out at an orange sun slung low and large in the dusk; grass barely stirs and the rooms are only now cooling down. The house has been renovated since my husband's childhood summers and it is as if that renovation has altered the weather, the air. The house's walls are curved and gentle: I feel the handprint in the labour that has rounded the edges of the wooden counter, see the movement of an arm in swooping plaster crescents on the ceilings. Everything is beautiful, from the décollaged vinegar bottle to the hand-painted water glasses. It is not just being away from my usual space, not just the views of sea and mountains beyond every window, that prompt me to write: it is the house itself. Something here moves me to think about my parents' stories, to try to put them into words. Perhaps it is because I am gazing towards the Atlantic, aware of all of the Irish emigrants who crossed it in desperation or desire. Perhaps it is because I have never before been away by myself with the children, and have a heightened awareness of my own role as a parent. As I opened the house and drew back heavy curtains from picture windows, it felt as if I was peeling back something in myself.

*

My mother regularly punctuated stories about people or places she encountered in New York with the same ending: it would make a great play, wouldn't it? or a novel? She was proud of her Irishness and endlessly curious about other immigrants' lives and experiences. A gifted actress with an enormous capacity for empathy, she could see the drama in all things, from the resigned tristesse of a Pakistani cab driver who once drove her home from the opera, to the long-time doorman's progress in converting his Queens home to accommodate a doddering aunt born in the Dominican Republic. She never acknowledged the extent to which her own stories were dramatic and deserving of empathy.

*

In the evenings in Mayo I feed the children, my eyes moving between their faces and the sea beyond the windows. We eat simply here in this holiday space: raw veggies, hummus; I toast brown bread with sharp cheddar under the grill and there are bowls of strawberries and blueberries. The baby still like a bird opening his mouth for the spoon, angling for his brother's attention, smiling toothily. Their small faces rouse endless, unspeakable feeling in me. The first night I'd envisioned enjoying the rare luxury of a bed to myself, but I'd quickly abandoned the attempt to put them to sleep in a separate room. After an hour of writing I'd spent two more continuously lulling one and then the other child back to sleep – my patient son's eyes dream-full as he was woken again and again by his panicking small brother. Instead, each night I now lie on my side feeding the baby in the king-sized bed, my older son beyond him. I sing while their hands cling to what they can reach of my body, nestled into my shoulders, my neck, twisting locks of hair round fat fingers. When they are fast asleep and I can slide my nipple from the baby's mouth, I crawl towards the light in which I can write, always pausing in the doorway to look at them, so small in the bed, their breathing beginning to align. Once asleep in this way, they rarely wake or even stir. They both know I will return; they seem to accept this interim time when they are alone but together.

Some nights – not many, but a memorable few – I do not write. I sit instead at a stool at the kitchen counter with a small tumbler of wine. I watch the sky and grieve for lost ideas, for the inability to find words, for all the places I was not born, including this one, this tiny townland on Clew Bay. I have no familial or historical attachment to this place, but it has lured me in. I grieve because in these instances, with the children fast asleep, I am alone in a beautiful house, and beautiful houses always evoke in me an indefinable longing.

*

When my parents married, they were given a house by my paternal grandfather. It was not the gift of a rundown building on a farm, or the necessary gift so many generations received of being allowed to reside with their elders. It was, instead, a brand-new house, a showhouse replete with all the extras that the builders had thought to add: cunning cupboards, a pantry artfully shelved, a window seat in the marital bedroom.

I was never in it, their first marital home. I peered at it on Google Maps once, the place I should have been born. Constructed as an upmarket enclave in a charming village, it is now surrounded by development and major roads in Churchtown; ringed by apartment buildings, the cluster of mid-twentieth century houses seems irrelevant. On one occasion, when my mother and I were in the car with my oldest son and realized we were near, we circled towards it and drove slowly by. My mother was then nearing eighty. She did not cry, just shook her head. No need to stop, she said quietly. I think we both felt the quick exposure to other lives: a shiver flew through me as we pulled away.

*

I grew up instead in an apartment building in New York, one of four towers in a gorgeous complex on the East River near the United Nations. It was an aspirational partnership between the city and investors aimed at creating a community, with acres of pedestrian space that included playgrounds, gardens, seating areas, a riverwalk and a private promenade suspended between the buildings. There was also an indoor swimming pool and health club, a grocery store, salon, dry cleaners, bank, two nursery schools, a bus stop. It remains, in my memory and in fact, a picturesque retreat in the midst of Manhattan. We lived there because my father happened to be at the Actors' Equity office in New York when a flyer was put up about this new complex: while three buildings were free market, some spaces in the last were to be based on income, and artists and actors were encouraged to apply. My mother said that it was like winning the lotto, getting word that they had been successful in their bid for an apartment there. But it was rental-only, something that, as I got older and learned that other people owned their homes, made it seem as if all of the stability the place afforded could be swept away. That it was built on reclaimed land began to hold sway in my imagination, despite the fact that the foundations were drilled into the bedrock below the river: I lay in bed and felt the lack of solid ground.

*

When the children and I return to the house from the beach each afternoon, my oldest son builds Lego or draws detailed pictures of the harbour while the baby naps in sea-air exhaustion. Since there is no internet here and the phone signal is weak, it's at this time I stand in a corner of the dining room to read and reply to messages. Donal is amazed by my insistence that the weather is lovely and can't wait to see it for himself at the weekend. He misses us and I feel badly that he can't be here during the week as well: I send him a slew of pictures. I thumb a brief email to my mother in New York, attaching photos of the children on the beach that morning, the sand around them scuffled by spades: they are gleaming with water and joy and I know she will relish their delight. My friend Nancy has asked how the writing is going and filled me in on when she'll arrive in nearby Achill with her husband and daughter. Nancy is one of my two American friends in Ireland; like me she immigrated after falling in love. Since we met, we have been in constant touch, seeing each other during our children's regular playdates. I text her how much I love this place and she replies *I told you so* because she is already obsessed with Mayo and particularly Achill, with the stone walls of the west of Ireland, the placid sheep, salty air, artists' studios. She is an artist herself, a singer-songwriter and craftsperson. We plan for an upcoming sunny day at Keem Beach with our mutual friend and I put the phone away. Good luck with the novel: you got this! reads Nancy's last text.

*

The Chinese woman on the twenty-sixth floor of our New York apartment building cared for the motherless daughter of a wealthy Hongkonger, her own children back in mainland China without her. To earn extra money for her family, she prepared and sold dumplings while her charge was at school. She always delivered them herself, he could perform with receipts, ticket stubs and whole shoeboxes of evidence he stored up through the year. The table strewn with these things and my father rapidly shifting items from one pile to another, my mother despairing at the state of the living room. I thought his interest a curiosity, never imagined it had been a profession.

My mother wouldn't tell me how he'd lost the insurance job, but it was something shameful, she said.

A fraudulent claim? Money missing? My mind worked. All she would tell me was that after he'd been fired, he continued to go out of the house as if for work, day after day, for several months.

That first morning: the sadness of rising out of bed and entering into the new role – insurance agent, happily married, Ireland, 1959. The performance of a lifetime.

*

When Dublin rents during the boom began to rise beyond our ability to pay them, Donal and I had managed to buy a small field in Wicklow with an old cabin in it, the only place we could afford. I was waitressing and Donal had delivery shifts while we were finishing degrees; we were not obvious candidates to buy property. But banks played loose with mortgages then and we found ourselves standing on our own bit of ground. We told ourselves we would build a proper house later. In that old cabin, despite leaks, mushrooms growing in clutches in the bathroom window frame, despite the ancient bathtub and its rubber-hosed shower, despite the fact that

I couldn't yet drive, I slept deeply, finally free of something. It was as if a long-time ringing in my ears had resolved itself and I could hear silence again. In the house in Mayo, I experience something similar: something in me quietens and images from the past unfurl.

*

There was a divorced couple whose children shuttled between their two apartments on the fourteenth and seventeenth floors, using the stairs, skipping the elevator. The children moved depending on seasons, arguments, hormones – bumping suitcases up and down between their parents' places, metal fire doors echoing behind them.

*

Not long after marrying my father, my mother was told that she could not have children. They performed exploratory surgery, she told me, but it didn't work; they found nothing wrong, but she had no child, year after year. My child's hands felt the delicate scars on the soft skin of her belly: I was perhaps seven, horrified at the idea of surgery, a concept beyond childhood's shelter from knives and sharp items. Poor Mommy, I said.

But then I had you, she said triumphantly. I can still hear that note in her voice, its sledgehammer swing back at the doctor, at an Irish medical establishment that never dreamed of asking whether there were any issues with the husband. Having accepted that she'd never have children, it didn't occur to her that the sickness and swelling of that 1970s spring meant a baby. Only when she went to a doctor out of concern that she might have a cancerous growth in her stomach did she find out that she was pregnant.

*

I pour words onto the screen in the evenings in Mayo, feeling caught in its glow as a spotlight.

When a friend gave me Gaston Bachelard's *The Poetics of Space* in my twenties, I read it on the subway up and down to work, dumbstruck by his articulation of the cocoons that are our homes as children, of our need to nestle, enclose ourselves, make the world small enough to manage. In the rattling carriage I gazed through the windows at the dark walls of the tunnels peeling past and know that he was right.

Something of that child must remain in me because as I write of distant events and people, I wish for a nest, a shell, a cocoon.

*

My best friend Becky and her family also lived on twenty-six and had their own story: of marriage between the daughter of Irish Catholics and the son of Polish Jews. From their windows, Becky pointed out Queens and Brooklyn, where her mother and father had been born. This astonished me, that their birthplaces were visible from here, that they had family so nearby. In lieu of the pointing, I showed Becky photos of my parents in Ireland, and Becky showed me slides of her parents in India, where her dad had been in the Peace Corps. In this way we examined the evidence of our parents' pasts.

When Becky's parents sought a weekend home in the country, I was sometimes present on the drives. We played *I spy* in the backseat with Becky's sister Emily for a while, pressing Silly Putty against comics so that the newsprint image was visible on the putty and we could stretch and distort it. The windows were open and Becky's fine honey-gold hair flew around her face: I could see the static in its straight lines. Emily's was short after a self-inflicted haircut and hardly stirred, while my own hair whipped into my mouth when I laughed. Out of the city the landscape opened up in ways that surprised me: the absence of tall buildings, the presence of cornfields. I remember asking questions about the styles of architecture, enamoured with the language of the descriptions. Becky and I talked about the places we passed, assessing them according to our tastes. I came to favour saltbox over A-frame, shingle over slate, though the house-hunting was none of my affair.

*

The retired gay men on the second floor swam together each morning in identical shorts, their tanned skin giving notice of Florida winters. They were one of few couples I knew in New York in which both partners were American, if from different parts of the country. When one died of a heart attack on the pool's edge, the other never swam again. I was a teenage lifeguard when I returned locker contents to their apartment months later. At first the widower could not place me – out of the lifeguard chair and my neon-yellow uniform – but then the trauma of that day flashed over his face. I wished I hadn't come. I noticed that his tan had faded and hoped I conveyed sympathy in the way that I lifted the cloth bag and its contents up to him, an offering.

*

When Donal and some of his relatives arrive at the weekend in Mayo, the routine I'd established in the holiday space disappears. I can go for a proper run in the morning and hit my stride with Donal there to mind the children, but I cannot gaze silently at the sea all evening after our children are asleep. The weather was never so beautiful in all the years Donal and his family spent summers here. They're in holiday mood, elated by the current weather. The sun is shining now so they can laugh about their previously sodden vacations. They talk about the summer when, after the first week, their dad drove to Westport to hire a TV. Horizontal rain swept the views away and they spent several days watching Wimbledon in and out of focus before deciding to go home. The last straw was a miserable walk up Croagh Patrick in thick wet mist.

I sit by and try to smile at the right moments. I'm in the swirl of my own thoughts. I am still trying to write about the painful nature of my parents' past, though fiction is failing me. In these moments my focus is so internal, so elsewhere, that it is challenging to turn outward again. I make excuses: alone with the children on my own all week, the broken sleep of breastfeeding, co-sleeping. They nod in understanding. Donal's arm circles my shoulder protectively, ushering me back to the lived reality of adults. Our oldest son tells them, to much amusement, about my laps around the house. But I don't want more than to run in circles, to stay close to this house that contains our children, this house that brings me such peace.

*

On the twenty-second floor there was a Bangladeshi family whose teenaged daughter passed for Puerto Rican at school and got kicked out of the apartment when her parents realized what she had done. In later years she came back to visit, a small daughter in tow whose sneaker laces stood in bright white rows.

*

When Nancy arrives in Mayo, we meet on the beach with our friend Aoife, who is also holidaying nearby. Our clatter of children shriek at the small waves, urging each other into a giggling frenzy as they attack the fringes of the water in unison before a ragtag retreat. The tension of writing about my parents relents. The writing is hard, but Donal is here; we are on the beach with dear friends and our children with their outrageous vivacity. It had been amid the same noisy children, with the same friends, that I'd taken a call to say that my first novel would be published. When Nancy, Aoife and I had ourselves shrieked after I'd told them the news, the children stopped dead to stare at us, grown women laughing and hugging in the garden outside the home that Donal and I had eventually built to replace the leaking cabin.

*

One birthday, a dollhouse arrived. I disappeared into it: there are details of those rooms I recall more vividly than my childhood apartment. The buying of furniture and items for the house became a long-term preoccupation for everyone in my family. Designs of miniature sets for my dad's shows moved in. In a Pennsylvania antique shop I spotted an oak and velvet trundle bed, thick with dust, and pleaded with my mother to trade upcoming weeks of allowance to be allowed buy it. One Christmas my father spent hours with a tiny generator, wiring minute lamps for the rooms. My mother sewed finicky dolls' clothes, knitted blankets, hemmed sheets.

I spent whole days so immersed in my dollhouse that returning to the normal-sized world disquieted me; I went to bed in the not-dark of New York City and the dolls carried on in my mind. Usually I fell asleep staring towards my dollhouse. The electric doll-fire was made of crackled orange glass with a flickering bulb behind it, and the dolls perched on sofas, their perpetually flat feet resting on deep, soft rugs.

My friends drew people and cats, dogs and horses, flowers and rainbows. I sketched houses, rooms, writing notes to myself around the edges. I didn't like the *Archie* comic books that Becky favoured; I took the copies of *Architectural Digest* that my mom brought home from the office into my room and pored over them.

Later, when I was in my twenties and working at a university in a new city where I didn't know anyone, I spent the autumn and winter evenings talking on the phone to Donal in our faraway cabin and then putting myself to sleep in my rented room with stacks of literature from the university's architecture library. Sometimes

I awoke in the middle of the night because I'd wedged myself uncomfortably against the outsize coffee-table books; sometimes I dreamed I was in a mid-century modern house back in Arizona where my parents had once lived before I was born, or had nightmares that I was tasked with shingling an endless undulating roof, cedar resin impeding the work. My fingers stuck together and to the tiles themselves. I tried and tried to shake them off, never succeeding.

*

There is something that I try to explain to myself about the meaning of my parents' lives and cannot. It has something to do with the fact that, after generations of life in Sandymount and a surprising lack of emigration in her family, my mother's narrative swerved with my father's. And that swerve was also, powerfully, mine. As a result I would never belong to a particular place: I would always be the child who heard of 'home' as something far off in place and time. I would be the visiting relative with the different accent, the different language, the relative who lived in a rented apartment and was surprised to learn that it was possible to *buy* the places where one lived.

I would always be uneasy, hoping that I was smiling in the right places.

Several years later, when we are staying in Mayo once again and Donal and I are alone in the kitchen looking at darkening Clew Bay, I tell him how aware I am of being the only one left in my family. He is offended. We are your family, he tells me. He soothes me. But the next day, when he describes an event of his childhood, he says 'we' unthinkingly. I can't quite explain to him my sense that I had never been part of a 'we'. This is the rupture of forced emigration and shameful departures.

*

On a scorching day out at Westport House, Nancy, Aoife and I are stuffed alongside our kids into a tiny train that chugs us through the grounds. The kids whoop and wave at everyone we pass. We picnic in the grounds and the day passes in a haze of heat, fun-fair rides. I don't think about writing at all; I don't think about how hard the book is to write. Instead I am wiping tears from my eyes, my face aching from chronic laughter.

*

There was a garrulous producer on thirty with Irish connections who married a famous actor when her child was almost grown up. She valued her Irish heritage, romantic in its abstraction, and running into my mother or even to me accelerated her conversation. Sometimes she rhapsodized about a place she'd researched for vacation – Doolin, Tralee – or sang snippets of popular Irish songs, including U2. In the elevator, the woman and the actor were drunk and too full of gesture in such a small space, in need of a larger platform.

*

My parents were six years married when my father gambled away the house his father had given them. As a result, they left their lives in south Dublin and emigrated to the United States, where, eventually, I would be born. The loss of the house was not the first loss, though my mother didn't know that. First, my father had lost his insurance job. She didn't tell me about the house and the job at the same time, because it had been too overwhelming for her, I think, to hear it in one fell swoop. He hadn't told her himself; he'd gone to her father, who listened and nodded and didn't react, knowing that he would have to help his daughter to hear this dreadful news, and then to bear it.

I see them: my broken father and his gentle, stalwart father-in-law, driving to the house they no longer owned. And though it is over sixty years since then, though I wasn't yet alive when the events took place, I feel both the shame and the despair; I feel how that moment has continued to ripple through days and decades.

*

I learned what had happened to my parents' first house around the time I left the US to move permanently to Ireland, when my father was long dead. Once I knew, I kept imagining dramatized versions of the house being gambled away. In my mind it was a Western saloon out of the old movies: swinging doors at the entrance, a horse or two in the sunlight beyond. My father at a round table in his 1950s' Irish clothes, a suit, a tie. His wedding ring wasn't on his finger – it seems to have been merely a prop – but I noted its absence as I did when a child. The others at the table were stereotypical cowboys, hats atilt and weather-ruined skin.

I'll see your fifty cents and I'll raise you one living room complete with three-piece-suite, walnut sideboard and fire irons, assorted tasselled lamps.

Master bedroom with fitted wardrobes and views of the Dublin mountains.

Additional bedrooms to be filled by yet unborn children.

Kitchen, pantry.

Acreage, drive.

I always averted my mind when it came to my father, tie loose now to battle a choking sensation, walking slowly towards the doors and returning to my mother, who is as yet unaware that the house was no longer theirs. I could never bear to watch. As with those old movies, I switched the channel.

*

Had everything gone to plan, I'd have been far older than I am now. It was two decades before I appeared in my parents' marriage, the opposite of their lost house.

*

The drives to look at houses with Becky and her parents were through New Jersey and Connecticut, upstate and into Pennsylvania. Becky and her younger sister sometimes squabbled in the car and from the peace-maker seat in the middle, my eyes took in the swiftly passing houses, picket-fenced or open-lawned, suburban or rural; weathered wooden boards, flag poles, basketball hoops. One place we seemed to pass often had a stream looping across a green lawn. There were tiny footbridges at either end of the house, and I imagined living there, the novelty of the moat.

The place Becky's parents eventually bought was in a gated community called Silver Key Shores. The name mirrored my profound sense that to own a home was indeed to have a precious key. I didn't grasp at all what a gated community was, only felt excited each time we approached the barriers at weekends and a guy in a booth with a forest ranger-style hat let us in. Not only was it a gated community, but the lake was man-made. I was intrigued: how had such a large lake been manufactured? The hole I could understand, but the water? How could something be made out of nothing?

I spent many weekends with them, enough to recall which presses the mugs and plates were in, the porch view in different seasons; to have seen a bear rummaging in the bins, deer demolishing the young fruit trees Becky's father had so carefully planted. Sometimes my parents were invited, too. There is a picture of them at the lake in summer, flushed with sun, unhappy, overexposed. I remember feeling that I enjoyed the weekends there more on my own, too awkward to manage being myself in the manufactured American landscape and being their daughter all at once.

*

The cliché is that children are concerned with their parents' lives only so far as those lives directly concern them, unable to imagine that their parents have thoughts, emotions, experiences that extend beyond their own. Maybe this is true for some – I don't know. But within my earliest memories, I can hear my parents' voices telling me about the long before, the two decades of marriage that preceded my presence. I couldn't possibly stand up to that dramatic twenty years. It seemed such a long time to me as a child, always a multiple of my age: a whole lifetime, much more than I could grasp. Confronted with calculus in high school, I would feel the same bafflement. So I acquired a reverence for the time before as well as a dread of it, puzzling to understand it, to sum things up.

*

One morning before we had children, Donal and I called into his parents' house for a chat, something we did regularly. The post had just arrived and my father-in-law opened a bank statement as we sat around the kitchen table together. He held the piece of paper up for us all to see, beaming: their mortgage was paid off. We toasted the event with coffee and biscuits. This, their family home, had a story behind it. Towards the end of the nineteenth century, a Wicklow builder designed a house for himself. It was in the manner of a Victorian dollhouse, with a porch and intricately carved fascias painted white, which appeared like icicles dangling off the red-tiled roof. He added a carriage house and hired an arborist to design a garden – unusual at the time for a self-made man of his class. The original garden designs survive, as do many of the trees, including a soaring tulip that produces cradling hands of petals. The young builder never moved into his house, however. He fell in love with an engaged woman, who fell in love with him, too, and broke off her engagement. Her jilted fiancé promptly sued the builder under chattel law and was awarded the beautiful house with its walled gardens. Some of the court documents were among the deeds and garden plans when my in-laws bought the property two generations later.

My in-laws had lived in three houses up to that point in their married life, and the confiscated house was the first on which my mother-in-law was named as co-owner, after thirty years of marriage.

My own mother's name was not, of course, on the house's deeds when my parents married, was not on the deeds when the house was lost.

*

At the house in Mayo by the sea, Donal and the children try to surprise limpets off rocks for crab-fishing. The limpets hear them coming over the sand at low tide and cling hard. In place of limpets we tie rasher rinds to twine and lower them into the water from the pier's edge. The tiny crabs that the children swing onto the concrete are furious and hasty, running sideways towards the drop back into the shallows. I hold the baby and think of how next year, he will want to do this himself: he will insist, toddler fashion, in holding his own line, and I will have to hold fast to his jumper, his trousers, to keep him from following the crabs.

I am always unnerved by this game, even though the limpets have been excused a role and the crabs are merely examined in sand buckets full of water before being returned to the sea. Their dark green shells are so mottled that when they are underwater they are difficult to see. Captured by their own eagerness for food, their splayed legs swill through the water until they reach the bottom of the bucket and cease moving, playing dead. Returned to the pebbled pier, they immediately dash towards the edge, their tiny eyes evidently showing the way. I watch them with their houses on their backs and say aloud that the wind is getting up, that perhaps it's time to think about tea.

*

When my grandfather died my father and his sister discovered the house they had grown up in was rented. My grandmother may have known, but she had died years before when the children were small. The shock was great, since renting among his class at the time was highly unusual, and everyone was puzzled: why would so wealthy a jeweller never have bothered to purchase his home? There was no house to sell. My father and his sister divided the savings and the jewellery, and sold the business that neither was suited to.

Given that my father was already experiencing money difficulties, though he had yet to lose the house, the lack of a property in his inheritance was likely a major blow. It is hard to think of him alongside my favourite literary scoundrels who squander away funds, keep secrets, increasingly turn to alcohol for succour. I do not want him in their company, and I think that is one of the reasons that I began to write the novel – to retrieve him, straighten his collar, help him face the facts of his past:

and, of course, to write a different ending. But the novel fails, year after year, the fictional construct never capturing some essence of my parents' immigration stories.

*

My mind rejected the saloon scene as I got older. But how did one gamble away a house, I wondered, if not in that dramatic fashion? Room by room? Square metre by square metre?

The truth of gambling away an entire house was likely extremely prosaic, I imagined: my father, out of work, may have approached a bank. A small mortgage advanced on a mortgage-free house would be no problem; he was sure to find another job. The sum fluttered away on drinks, rounds in the pub, Christmas presents, perhaps the odd bet on a horse, a friendly card game – for he was not a gambler, only generous and used to being so. The true bets were, I suspected, ones he placed against himself, losing again and again.

No new job turned up. The months went by. The loan went unpaid and collectors were called in. This image replaced the saloon scene in my mind: the showhouse was now in the possession of the bank, my mother pale in the front room among the wedding gifts that remained on display.

*

On foot of visa sponsorship by a wealthy couple they agreed to work for as domestics, my parents left Ireland for Seattle. But then, as winter beckoned in the north, they followed their employers away from snow on Mount Rainier – away from rain pooling on the Pike Street

Market cobbles; away from the mansion on the sound with its guest houses, pier and gates – to a *ranch*, a term that couldn't be used in Ireland for any house or stretch of land. Arizona was different. If Ireland was grey and green and eggshell-white and, sometimes, vivid, aching blue when the sky was scoured free of clouds, this place was yellow and sandy and emaciated blue and rust and tawn and no green at all, no grey at all: only my mother's eyes and my father's hair.

The town nearest the ranch was not on the map, even in Arizona. The first year they flew down, along the Cascades until they gave way to chasms. When their employers left in their car, for occasional weekends at first and then for an extended sojourn to their other ranch in Mexico, my parents were alone.

There was no one there.

They were servants, caretakers. This was long before *The Shining*, and anyway there was no child. But they were swarmed by the feeling of containment, of not being able to go anywhere. My mother had a guitar my father had bought for her, and each day after the various chores and maintenance that needed to be done she would sing and play. She was at odds with the landscape, her dark hair and cream complexion set against the sandscape of yellow, the skyscape of blue. The songs she sang, they too were at odds: 'Danny Boy' in the clarity of the air and stark light, the notes unused to such exposure. She missed so violently the music of her childhood and her home: the piano, the record player with its stock of opera; the deep hum of her double bass in the school orchestra against the tenor of her sister's cello; the warm-up notes of her brother, now living in Germany and teaching music; the pedals of the organ that her aunt, great-aunt and great-great-aunt had played in Star of the Sea, the Sandymount church. It was a vanishing, the way that the music stopped.

She persisted, and learned new chords, new songs. Joan Baez, Bob Dylan: in the voice that won the Feis Ceoil medal, the one that had starred in every school musical; the one that had given her a career in Irish theatres. Until this. Now, in Arizona, she was a maid, a cook, a caretaker, general mender, and the guitar was a hobby, something meant to stave off insanity, the jungle of it in the desert.

*

At the annual plaza festival each summer, Vietnamese diplomats who lived in several apartments scattered through the building set up a food stall with spring rolls and mung-bean cake. They crouched down to hand these delicacies to small children like me with gentle smiles. If the line for food wasn't long, they sometimes showed us intricately painted water puppets and described the performances. Their presence at the festival was at odds with the protestors regularly encamped beyond the lobby in the late 1970s, angrily shouting about American MIAs from within cages constructed of bamboo poles. Towards the end of high school my friend Amy's father, bringing out the garbage on the thirty-sixth floor, found several sacks of letters that the diplomats had put in the recycling pile. Each one – in varying tones – asked about a relative who had never returned from the war and wanted assistance that the diplomats could not provide.

*

My father did not miss the music. He busied himself with house-painting, the mending of fences. It was the old saw, the one that believed in busyness to ward off indulgence, and it worked for him. In Arizona, there was no pub; there was no one to drink with. There was nothing to bet on – the rain would stay off in the far north, the sun would rise tomorrow and it would be hot. And so the desert suited him. A photograph of him: shirtless, brown, sunglassed, a paintbrush in his hand, happy.

My mother suffered for the transgressions of her husband, found herself cast far beyond even her imaginings of what it meant to be in America. The only reprieve came on Sundays, when a Hopi man named Jude appeared in a ramshackle pick-up truck. The first time he arrived my mother paused in her work watering plants beneath the veranda, hearing the truck before she could see it. She ran for my father, feeling trapped in a Western, sure they were to be murdered. My parents stood together in the shade of the porch watching the snake of dust kick up behind the truck.

When their employers had taken off for their second ranch in Mexico they'd told Jude, a long-time friend, about my mother and father. And so Jude befriended my parents, kindly drove the hour and a half from town each week, bringing them to Mass at a church peopled mostly by Hopi and Mexicans. My parents remained in town for the day, shopping, walking around, socializing, after a time, with Jude and his family and friends. Then as the sun began to set he drove them back to the ranch with their groceries, newspapers, and renewed faith.

Maureen, my mother, as he drove away: waving, not crying, not crying, not crying.

*

Each time we are by the sea in Mayo, as the years pass, I think of my parents. There is something about this house, positioned on edge of land and water, that rivets my mind to the liminalities of our familial existence. The players in the drama are all dead, my father gone so long that I count the time in decades, my mother gone long enough that I've begun to miscalculate the number of years. When we pack to return home to Wicklow, we bundle wetsuits and boogie boards, towels and beach treasures into the car. On a sideboard we leave the best beach find of that summer – one yellowy sand dollar, perfect and whole – atop tiny thank-you drawings by the children. I lift the heavy curtains back into place to shut the house away, brush the last of the sand from the floor. While the children fly around on the grass outside, I walk barefoot through the rooms one final time to make sure we have unplugged the refrigerator, left no food or beloved toys. Then I pause before each painting and tapestry on the walls, because while the house has prompted a confusion of memories, it has also provided a space to write about them, and it is difficult to leave. Donal takes one child, I take the other, and we drive home.

*

After two years of working for their American visa sponsors, my parents were free to remain in the US and to return to theatre work. In Seattle they bought a house on Queen Anne Hill: an open-plan, split-level with a wraparound deck and both their names on the deed. My mother created a Japanese garden; they adopted a Siamese cat and named it Fionn Mac Cumhaill. They lived in that house for several years before my father was offered enough theatre work on the east coast that they began to talk of moving to New York. In the end they decided to see how New York would go; he flew east to begin rehearsals and my mother was left to pack up the house, which she refused to sell, agreeing only to rent it out. Believing they would be back she boxed up all the letters from home since she'd left Ireland and put them in the attic, comforted by the fact that for this move she did not have to sell things. She packed carefully, putting the letters into boxes, taping them shut. She stored most ornaments, paintings, knick-knacks – bringing only what they would need in the new apartment (still to be found) in New York; in the meanwhile, my dad slept on a friend's couch. Clothes she stuffed into bags and suitcases, gradually filling the car to capacity. When there was still some room, she skipped up the ladder to the attic and considered what else to take, deciding on a few more kitchen items and a portrait of her in oils, a Christmas present from my father that he'd asked her to bring if she could. She placed the painting behind the driver's seat, protecting it with a quilt.

On a Monday morning she handed the keys to their new tenants in the driveway, climbed into the turquoise Chevrolet brimful of the accumulation of America in her life and drove north. She reached Vancouver by late morning and went straight to the train station, checking the car in well ahead of time and even watching as it was driven up a ramp onto a carriage.

For three nights she slept in the tiny compartment as the train took her across North America to New York. Everything was miniaturized: bathroom, sink, pillows. It was a kind of marvel to her, a playhouse of sorts. She relished the morning ritual of folding sheets and blankets, stowing them in the purpose-built compartment and transforming the bed into a settee. Decades later, she would take me on an overnight train from Madrid to Paris, remembering aloud curtains withheld by snaps – so ingenious – and extraordinary views, the endless parade of changing landscapes as she went east across the Rockies: the mountains collapsing into plains, valleys, towns, cities, all merging into a stream as the train unzipped the landscape, hour after hour. She was amazed by the thick clusters of stars at night.

There was a reading carriage, and each day she spent hours there chatting, mostly with retired Canadian couples taking their time to go cross country at a leisurely pace. *The actress*, as she became known, even sang a song one evening after dinner as the train clattered away from sunset.

She would never spend a night in the house on Queen Anne Hill again, and sold it just before my father's death. When she climbed into the attic to retrieve her letters, which marked the distance from her family week by week, they were gone, no trace of them amid the junk that was left.

*

Back at home in Wicklow I email an old family friend who was in the theatre with both of my parents in the fifties and early sixties. I ask questions I never asked my parents, who are gone now. Maybe I sound desperate because I receive a reply that is unexpectedly detailed about my parents' fractured marriage in the time before they left for America. Here is a source from which I might learn the truth, so I write again: what had my father done to lose his job and house?

There was no crime, no offence but his addiction: spotted at a pub every lunchtime for a week and suspected of being regularly drunk at work, he was fired. The truth is often this prosaic. And in a small city, everyone heard, everyone knew. Small borrowings mounted, and the house fell.

*

The Irish couple on the seventh floor were actors who had one daughter, born unexpectedly after they'd been married for twenty years.

*

My parents never spoke of where they lived between the time the showhouse was repossessed and when they left for the States. I see them drive straight to the airport, slipping the silver key tarnished with six years' use back in through the letter box, leaving the car at Dublin Airport as if they'd be back soon.

INDIVIDUAL WILLS

There's a non-existent film of my parents playing opposite one another as Gabriel and Gretta Conroy. They were about thirty and still living in Seattle when it was made, so perhaps about the same age as the couple in 'The Dead'. It was shot on film, with all of the resultant anxiety that there might be a hair on the gate or that the loader would have a mishap. And then there was the fact that they were stage actors and had to adjust to the new lights, to the breaking down of a scene into such small segments that there was sometimes inane repetition when a retake was required.

Gabriel says everyone wears them on the continent.

Gabriel says everyone wears them on the continent.

Gabriel says – until it seemed not Joyce but Beckett, my father said:

Thirty-nine today, sound as a …

Thirty-nine today, sound as a bell, apart from my old weakness …

The make-up still thick but the lights hotter.

My mother wore her own shoes and earrings. The dress was from the Rep, one she'd worn in Chekhov the previous season. My father wore a dapper suit with a London label. It was also a part of the Rep's collection, heavy with the sweat of the summer season, beautifully made.

It wasn't too many months after my father had gone off the rails again, so they had been through the terrible silence of the first week, through rows and then recovery. My mother had insisted, for the first time, that he do something about it: go to AA, she told him coldly in the garden one morning. She was weeding flower beds and watching for her raccoon; despite warnings she'd befriended one who came regularly and now took food from her hands, standing up on its hind paws like a dog. There are other actors there, she told him without looking up. It was the power of being in her own house. In her own house – her name on the loan – she spoke up.

My father agreed; what else could he do? Then the script had arrived, and they'd delightedly begun to rehearse: words to say, lines that could be practised at the table when the pain of silence was too much to bear.

The lure of theatre: to have someone else tell you what to say, how to act, who to be.

Were you dancing?

Of course I was. Didn't you see me? What row had you with Molly Ivors?

No row. Why? Did she say so?

Something like that. I'm trying to get that Mr D'Arcy to sing. He's full of conceit, I think.

There was no row, only she wanted me to go for a trip to the west of Ireland and I said I wouldn't.

Oh, do go, Gabriel! I'd love to see Galway again.

You can go if you like.

There's a nice husband for you, Mrs Malins.

Over dinner – always with water, never with wine – they say these things back and forth to each other until the wounding has gone out of them. The words begin to transform in that way that cannot be explained to lay people, to those who have not lived as somebody else in the dark beneath lights, with the still listening that is a rapt audience. They are now Gretta and Gabriel in the modern Seattle house with a fondue set on the table, the light of a hanging lamp a warm circle between them. It is an alchemy they do not discuss but seize on: tenderness between them again because they are not only themselves.

The shell of a carriage is brought onto set for the scene in which they journey towards the hotel. My parents sit in it, exposed on one side where the camera is angled invasively – it seems to be pointing the finger and they both recoil. They want to return to the rehearsal space of their dining-room table and the hanging lamp, that cocoon of light in which they can speak and perform only for one another. In the studio they do not even have the illusion of the utter dark that is the front of the stage, the blackness twinkling with dust hanging in the light like star particles.

The false carriage is surrounded by crew, so many of them, in jeans and short sleeves because of the heat: they hold booms and clipboards and watch intently. My parents begin, and they repeat the lines and look to one another and without speaking of it, without acknowledging the strange discomfort of this shoot, they disappear into the scene, into the characters; they are alone in the carriage and the beautiful glow of the wood puts sparkle in their eyes. They live Gretta and Gabriel in that strained journey to the hotel.

My father looks at his wife and he longs for her: and he knows that he is himself longing for Maureen as much as he is Gabriel longing for Gretta. Even though he does not say it, even though it is not part of the script, he thinks those words to himself: *moments of their secret life together burst like stars upon his memory*. She truly is so beautiful, and he turns his eyes upon her and thinks of their wedding day and her beloved face as she neared him in the church, the fear in her. He thinks of her weeping at different moments through the years and he wants to hold her against his heart and let her hear how those moments echo through him still, the constant tremble of regret. It is not part of the scene, though, and he does not move towards her, just looks – pours all of that longing and regret into it and hopes that she understands.

My mother has the harder role. Behind his head are the lights and a row of people all staring: she is vaguely conscious that it is her that they watch, the men and the women, her pale skin aglow in the hot lights and her eyes luminous.

You are a very generous person, Gabriel, she says. It was true; he was generous – he always had been. He would have shared anything he had. He'd presented spur-of-the-moment gifts not only to her but also to her family, nephews and nieces. He always had a pocketful of someone's favourite treat, lemon bonbons for her mother, an iced cherry loaf for her father. It was his way, an instinct of his – having always had money, it slid through his fingers like sand. It was how the house had been lost, of course, and how the odd drink had become bottles; the generosity extended towards himself as well. So Maureen-Gretta gazed at her husband with a sense of his limitation, his best trait. A smile curved her lips slightly, and Bernard-Gabriel smiled back.

When filming wrapped for the day they would sit together taking their make-up off. Outside the small dressing room the crew wrapped cables and returned lighting stands to corners for the next morning. My parents left together, waving to those still tidying the studio, often walked out by the director or a producer, everyone but my mother lighting cigarettes as the revolving doors nudged them onto the sidewalk.

Night, they'd all say, and stroll off as if the next day's shoot wasn't only twelve hours away. My father would take her hand as they walked and she would not pull away.

*

At some point in the eighties my dad contacted the TV station, but they'd destroyed the film. After he died, I wrote to some of their old theatre friends and someone sent me a slide of them on set in the carriage: a square of translucent image, the ghosts of my parents with light coming through them.

So I watch the non-existent film: I stare through the slide, held up to the window so that I see the vague green of the grass of my garden beyond, as if my parents are sitting there. There is something in me desperate to see this performance, to see them exchanging lines. If I can see the film, it will make sense of things. Because sometimes it is as if I have imagined the whole thing – our family life – as if I've made it up lying on my parents' bed staring at the ceiling, as if I am still four and in that hallucinatory state of pre-sleep, telling myself stories. But if I could hear them saying the words to each other, would I be able to bear it? The longing to see them again, together, is overwhelming at times. I wish that they could see their grandchildren, see that it is all okay: that things worked out in the end. That was, I think, what I wanted when I started that failed novel about them – an ending that made sense of things. I didn't know when I started it that it wasn't possible to rewrite or reimagine the past.

*

On the top shelf of a hall closet in our Manhattan apartment, stacked alongside a projector, were round cases of slides that represented my parents' lives before mine. The slide projector was fidgety, but as a child I was patient. The colours were odd, as if someone crayoned my parents' clothes, the sky and houses. The slides of Ireland were green like cartoon broccoli, the sea azure and dimpled.

I looked at them in their clothes from another time: bell bottoms and miniskirts, my mother's round sunglasses covering her small-boned face. Her hair in chignons, often twirled on her head so that her neck looked tender and young. My father had a beard a lot of the time, at the least a moustache, and was often smoking and grinning. They were beautiful and marked by lost glamour in the way that parents can be when you see them as having distinct lives, because they are not you and you clearly see that – their separation, their individual wills.

Other slides moved from Ireland to Seattle, then to Arizona. Things changed; the sky became a colour I didn't know in New York, a blue that was like marker; darker, bluer. I doubted its naturalness, suspicious of it as a trick of the camera, an accidental setting shift. But it was there again and again, as was the yellow sand and the orange rock and the pale green vegetation that was like you'd imagined it, faint and delicate; you could glance away from it and think you'd made it up for yourself, for comfort.

Mostly there were slides of my mother, fewer of my dad. These slides showed my father's perspective, then, on that new-to-them part of the world: that's what I saw. Whitewashed buildings intrigued him, as did adobe buildings, the beautiful orange brown. There were some landscapes, and then they petered out as if he needed to stop thinking about the expanses he was photographing, though perhaps he just got used to them. There were a few odd images that I scrutinized for ages, creeping closer to the projection on the wall and then back again for distance before realizing that the image showed a lizard on the ground, or a snake.

My mother in these images looked all wrong: against the doorway of a giant house she was pint-sized; sitting on a fence she looked like a child. It enfeebled her, that setting. The few slides of my father were also like images of a man I didn't know – he was so dark and smiling and so *outside*. There were no indoor slides, as if this period of their lives was a banishment to the wilderness, but one that my father enjoyed. He seemed to have exchanged shirts for a cowboy hat, slouched on his hair at a rakish angle; he had seized on this new version of himself.

I was – obviously – not in the picture: a fact that I found strangely comforting.

ALTHOUGH (ALTHOUGH) WE'RE APART

Instead of posting holiday cards, Nancy made a donation to a charity and sent emails in which she narrated highlights of their family year. To these emails she attached a song she'd recorded with her daughter: Nancy would play piano, guitar or ukelele and they would sing together. My favourite was their version of 'Tonight You Belong to Me', the plaint of the ukelele behind their voices, the sweet earnestness and perfect pitch of her small daughter's singing against her own lush vocals, held back so as not to overwhelm the beautiful childish voice:

My honey I know (I know)
With the dawn that you'll be gone
But tonight you belong to me.

On another occasion she recorded the same song with her mother, their voices similarly intertwining. Tears falling, I listen (again).

THEATRICS

My father, on his deathbed, had been wheeled into a new room. I found him there with my mother by his side. The room was nondescript but with a better view of the West Village, suggesting a thoughtfulness for those who visit with the dying. You could sit near the window and lose yourself in the geometrics of sky over the city, follow the rooves to particular landmarks, note absences and dips in the skyline – parks or squares or the demolition of an old building. Some moments it was as if you were looking at Edward Hopper paintings, others as if you were yourself in them. In the room where my father died, the gaze was continually directed outward; the city view demanded it. I held his hand, peered into his face and then, inevitably, gazed out at the sharp-angled rooftops, the strange circles of wooden water towers perched on tripods. I projected my father's death out into the city that he'd made his home, out over the buildings; then I scanned to him again, frail now in the bed, becoming insubstantial before my eyes. Back in the room there were still machines and wipeable surfaces, the intricate configurations of plugboards and sockets that mark hospital walls. What if I turned away to the cityscape and then found him gone when my eyes returned?

The following drawn-out hours of stretching breaths, and quiet exchanges between my mother and I, the occasional presence of a nurse, they felt fleeting, evaporative.

My father had already fallen into the state that precedes death: no longer speaking, eyes closed. My mother was crying a little. Unlike me she'd had nothing to eat since bringing my father to the hospital that morning. She'd come in with him for what we thought would be only routine blood tests following his recent diagnosis, but the day had changed. I insisted that I would run down and get her at a drink at least – but a kindly nurse heard our conversation and brought her tea and toast. It felt like an Irish gesture in the midst of Manhattan, some link to my father's past. But my mother couldn't eat; she sipped the tea instead and we sat there as my father's body began to labour and fail. By late afternoon, the city lights shimmered against the windows and the gaps between my father's breaths extended, pushing my mother into silence. It was as though she was holding her own breath. They had been married almost forty years by then, and though the half of the marriage that preceded my birth was obscured to me and the half I'd seen had often been a shambles, she had loved him deeply. Being present felt like an intrusion, yet she needed me there. They both did. I was the third point in our small triangle.

I had been born in that same hospital; perhaps my father had gazed out at the city's angles during my mother's long labour. They'd told me about those hours, drawn out as first births can be, marked variously by excitement, pain and boredom. I hadn't absorbed the meaning of the event for them, not really: what child does? I was still too young to understand with any fullness what it had meant for them to become parents, and later in life than was usual at the time. My father had been so nervous that it was my mother who'd driven to the hospital at those signs of imminent birth. After I was born, my father called family in Ireland from a payphone in the hospital lobby, jangling quarters and nickels into the slot, so excited he rang some people twice.

As I sat with him, I imagined him going home to sleep after my birth, leaving my mother and I here, driving the car through the city. He would not then have foreseen a return to this hospital to close out his life.

At one point I went in search of a nurse, wondering if he had already died. She returned with me, leaned over him and said, no, not yet, but soon. What I remember is that fact of not being sure, the strangeness of not being able to tell.

*

After he died my mother and I took a taxi home in the dark. We had been given a black plastic bag with my dad's scarf and coat, a pair of gloves stuffed into the pockets by his own hands. With this bag between us on the back seat, we spoke about the funeral as the taxi headed home through the traffic, because there was always traffic, even when someone had died. The driver's two-way radio sometimes crackled but he must have heard us. The hospital flag-down and the black bag had probably given it away already. The interior of the taxi was as generic as the inside of the hospital room, except for a miniature ornament in gold and red and yellow that dangled from the rear-view mirror.

What is that called? I asked the driver as I held the money through the window to the front seat.

Nettipattam, he told me. For decorating elephants in Kerala, my home place.

Unconnected to anything that had happened that day, the word *nettipattam* became an ornament in my vocabulary, something filigreed and delicate, not to be used.

*

When my father was diagnosed with cancer I was young, and cancer or heart attacks and such things all seemed abstract and distant; they were conditions that in my naivety and oblivion I thought happened to older bodies. I was at a literal distance when my father received his diagnosis, studying in Dublin, my parents in New York. I learned of his cancer in a phone box in Trinity Hall in Rathmines. It was November, dark and wet as I ran up the steps to the converted big house that then served as a reception building for the residence, where there were phone boxes with heavy glass panes. To those of my generation it goes without saying that these were the only two phones that we had the use of, their cables connected to receivers, the boxes attached to the wall. Each evening students, many foreign like me, formed queues, talking or reading while we waited. Using the phone then was a deliberate and engaged performance: a walk to the building, a queue, with specific change required, a number. When it was my turn I'd go in with my heavy fifty-pence coins and ring my mom at her office in New York; she would then ring me back immediately, dialling the number to whichever phone I was on.

But that day I called home, knowing that my dad was due to receive test results. Perched on a tall stool, I heard from my mother, first, about my father's diagnosis. Through the glass, while she spoke, I could see a German mature student who had just been telling me about how his reading of *Ulysses* was going; I could see his head was once again angled into the book. I responded to the news of my father's illness with the same practicality I'd exhibit the next month when he died. I asked about treatment, about how he was feeling. He was too upset to talk to me initially but then, hearing my mother answer questions on his behalf, he came on the phone. His voice was the same, though thicker with emotion. The queue through the glass was shorter than usual that evening, so I stayed on a few minutes more to be passed back to my mother, to hear further detail of what would happen. There would be no admission to hospital, but chemo was to begin immediately, the next day.

After the phone call the German student asked me how my parents were and I told him that my father had cancer, how strange it was to learn such a thing in a phone box, seeing the world I inhabited through the glass continuing on as usual. This was a stark reality that I was glad to suddenly comprehend: it could make things absurd, yes – as if I'd been inside a television looking out during the phone call – but was also comforting evidence of a continuum of time and place that would go beyond this moment. The German student nodded and told me how he'd been thinking about parallax in *Ulysses* and this chimed with my experience, how in the box I'd learned to see life (he said) from a different perspective, a different angle. Life was, after all, but an object. Or perhaps, I think now, it was a series of objects: books we were reading, semi-precious stones collected, even phone booths in which one spent small slices of significant time, learning the slink of the metal cable and hard plastic of the receiver by heart while hearing life-changing news.

The German student and I smoked a cigarette together (my father's diagnosis so remote from my own youthful existence). Then I went back to my room and wrote in a notebook about what I'd heard from my parents, gazing occasionally out of my window into the darkness with its flares of light.

I lived on the second storey of a low building that overlooked a small flat green within the walled grounds of Trinity Hall. There were lamp posts set along a path that led from the big house to our smaller annex, and the uniformity of the light from them resembled a poster of a Magritte painting that I had up on my wall, *The Empire of Light*. On certain rare days at particular times, when the grass held green from lingering daylight and the sky grasped blue but only just, the view, through the rectangular window, seemed to be this Magritte composition. It was day and night, night and day. Everything was very still. Things could be themselves, what they seemed, and also other things: they could be several things, everything at once, before and after.

My view could be the poster of the painting on my wall, the poster and the view side by side; I gazed at the poster the way I gazed at the view because it *was* a view. My view could also be the memory of standing before that painting and its companions in the Met in New York only months earlier, coming home to describe to my father how overwhelmed I'd been by Magritte, how I'd suddenly, newly thought about light, about the way it encased everything. He was sitting at our round dining table by the wall of living-room windows, one of which was slightly open despite the air-conditioning because he was smoking. When I came in he was reading but put the book aside to ask me about the exhibit, which he was also interested in but wouldn't likely see because he was busy with work and because, in September, it was his habit to take a week off and go to the US Open and watch the tennis; he'd also go on all of his days off. He listened to my enthusiastic report and asked about different paintings, about which part of the museum they'd put the exhibit in so that he could imagine it for himself. Together we admired the poster of the exhibit I'd purchased and planned to bring with me to college in Ireland.

The memory of that conversation was also part of my view in my room at Trinity Hall, a continent away, something only I could see, something that made the view recall Magritte all the more. Realizing that on one of those few days I might have gone to the US Open with him, the pang was sharp; he likely didn't ask because he suspected I would reject him, as I had other years, wanting instead to be with my friends, free of my parents.

In Ireland and away from my father as he moved into illness, I found memory becoming object. I gazed into the Magritte poster because it held many pasts for me. It allowed me to articulate memories to myself, though not yet in words, since there was no eulogy, not at that point, only the peculiarity of looking into past and future through the poster, the view of the darkened grass. I could not say. I could only wonder at the strangeness of life, the swarming of feelings, my own inability to articulate any of them. Instead I gazed at the view as a meditative object, dwelling on it in the endless way that I could at that age, at that time.

I kept thinking about the summer in New York, when I had spent more time with my dad than usual. I'd been home in late August and September because, instead of returning to Colorado for college, I was preparing to study in Dublin for the year. Most of my friends had returned to university so New York was quiet for me; and my summer job at a law firm had ended. I was reading classics – novels by Joyce, Flaubert, Lawrence, Tolstoy, Beckett – and visiting museums because it felt as if I was coming to: as if moving beyond the weird accelerations of my teenage years in the city was suddenly a possibility. I traded dive bars, pseudo relationships, pointless sex and the electric wastelands of New York nightclubs for solo trips to libraries and galleries.

Early autumn was gorgeous that year; the city orange-leaved, blue-skied. In the evenings my mother often had rehearsals or met her friend Joann to swim, so my dad and I sat together talking about books while he watched sports with the sound off or did the crossword and I experimented with making paper and hand-sewing books. It was strangely companionable and easy to sit with him alone then, when it hadn't been before. He was sober, I was no longer a child: we met in that pause before I left for Ireland. In the evening when the sun sank beside the Empire State Building we ate dinner and the living room was full of September light, pink and fierce on the white walls.

I thought of those weeks when I learned of my father's illness. Sitting there in my college room I saw, quite clearly, that my father would die from this disease, and assessed with the hard stare of a teenager what this prospect meant for him, for my mother. I was sad, but also unsurprised, because he'd been unwell for long enough. Here, at last, was a pronouncement that made sense of things. Here was a diagnosis that felt just, even, given the way in which he had lived: a type of cancer brought on by a robust twinning of drinking and smoking. Still young, I saw in stark terms. I sought reasons and causes and easily found them. It would be years, a decade, before I was capable of doing otherwise when it came to my father. I did not understand that the approaching loss would affect me, or how; I did not know that as the years passed

I would begin to see him from different perspectives and rue that he did not live long enough to know that. I would wish that the time during which we met as adults wasn't limited to those few weeks. Sometimes it feels as if only now, thirty odd years later, I would be able to stand up at his funeral and speak with compassion and love instead of out of the bitter disappointment that kept me from delivering a eulogy then.

*

For a while my father's cancer had not been cancer; it had merely been signals that he chose not to examine or interpret. A persistently sore throat, the smoker's cough. He didn't feel like eating things that he used to love. His stomach had become swollen despite his thin frame, but this was vaguely believed by my mother to be the result of the abuse his liver had coped with. With the inclination of other men of his generation, my father himself put his stomach ache down to indigestion, and chewed antacids. This is not a pipe, he seemed to say. At the same time it was, of course, cancer, but no one called it that in our apartment; it was just a smoker's cough, a voice over-extended by years of un-microphoned theatre work. It interested me that the flare of fear started in our stomachs at the word *cancer*; it was curious that this official naming of names precipitated emotion in a way that was wholly stereotypical and expected, and yet unavoidable. My father choked slightly on the phone, my mother had been tearful saying goodbye. I did not cry, but then I was in the booth looking out at the reel of my usual world, not in a room with my parents and this news, which writ large the disclaimer that life could change at any moment.

I did not cry. Perhaps it was because my parents signalled to me their concern that I was so far away, on my own, across the Atlantic, dealing with this news; I felt that they needed me to be okay. But it was also, of course, that I did not comprehend the seriousness of the situation, even as I knew that the cancer would kill him. My sense of time was staggeringly immature. I should not rush home, my parents said. My father was to undergo treatment in the coming weeks and it would be better if I remained in Ireland and continued my studies. So I would finish the term, travel to France, the Netherlands, Denmark and Sweden as planned, then return to New York for Christmas.

My father approved of this plan. He wrote me a letter describing a summer after he'd finished school in which he and a friend cycled across Belgium. He described towns rebuilt after the war, the remains of charming villages in which they camped. He had never before mentioned this trip, and after he died I thought that his diagnosis had probably engendered the realization that he had shared relatively little of himself with me.

I understood; the past was painful for him. When I was small, my mother told me that his childhood had been sad, that he had lost people he loved. Somehow she explained the death of his younger sister and his mother without terrifying me, and instead implanted a solid sympathy for my dad. In the albums my mother treasured there was a picture of my father with his mother, who wore glasses and a dress that appeared white in the colourless photo: she was smiling and holding her toddler about the waist while perched on a chair outdoors.

Another small square was of my dad and his dead sister, Patsy. They both wore knee socks, his dark and hers white with slightly frilled tops turned down. She had curling hair that must have been brown like his; my father's was cropped and he was missing teeth. The shape of their smiles was the same as they stood together, sides touching in evident camaraderie.

That wasn't there in a later photo of my father with his remaining sister, Geddie, who was older; he was an awkward teenager who had lost his mother and baby sister, and also the easy smile. One final photo of Patsy showed her on her own in a garden, head atilt, grinning. She'd evidently been told to pose and to stay still, as her arms are unnaturally straight and rigid by the sides of what looks like a party dress; a bow in her hair. It was the last photo that would be taken of her: *Patsy* was inked on the back in a hand not my father's – perhaps my grandfather's.

My mom and I studied those photos together, but my father did not want to join us. He never examined them with me, or in my presence: the albums were the preserve of my mother and me. I thought Patsy pretty and sunny and I felt terribly sorry for the little boy next to her who was my father and who had lost this sister; I also felt sorry for the tiny version of him with the teddy in one hand whose mother looked warm and good-humoured, smiling and possibly saying something to the photographer – her mouth slightly askew – while she kept her small son in reach. That had been his life, with these smiling people; and then they had died, young, awfully.

My mother's evident sympathy for him set a precedent that I followed until I was almost in my teens. By then I was angry with him, resentful of his drinking, protective of my mother whose life had been so changed by his alcoholism. In those years of being twelve, thirteen, fourteen, when my dad was in mounting physical crisis and on the cusp of being finally forced to stop drinking, I struggled to grasp why our family couldn't resolve this issue the way that all the American families surrounding us did: with separation or divorce. My mother would be happier, I sensed. I believed I would be.

I said as much to my mother once. I was at the Jersey shore with a friend and her mother for the week, tasting American life that was foreign to me despite my passport. During the day Jen and I lay on the beach and dove through waves and babysat the children of our host; in the evening we walked the boardwalk, went on rides, eyed other teenagers, smoked Marlboro Lights sitting on the dark beach listening to the edge of the ocean. It was a foreign space for us both, city girls who consumed greater America through TV ads and, in Jen's case, shows that I wasn't allowed to watch. I called home every other day from a public phone on the boardwalk near the house with its buckling mesh-screened porch, my feet in the fine sand and the sun-hot receiver pressed to my ear.

On one of the days my mother was upset, her voice constricted in some way that I recognized. I guessed that while she was talking my dad was passed out in bed. I asked why she let him stay. Why won't you divorce him? I demanded.

Because I could not live with myself if he ended up on the street, she told me. If he lost his job, or couldn't earn enough for rent.

The day was clammy, typical July weather on the east coast, with thunder forecast. It was as if the lightning struck early, because her words stayed in my ear, charging the air. I've made my choice, she said. I don't want him to suffer. I live with it and live my own life. Just as you need to live yours.

It was not a payphone conversation. I argued with her, told her that she was making that choice as an adult who had grown up in a loving household without dysfunction. I'm not choosing, I said. I don't get a choice.

Jen sat nearby on the sand, smoking and listening. Like all families we knew, hers was in its own complex situation and in her quiet waiting I sensed there were questions she might have asked too.

I was ashamed of him. But beneath that I was also ashamed of feeling that way, because I knew him to be an intelligent, gentle, loving man who, unlike other alcoholics I'd read or heard of, never shouted or became aggressive or angry. Instead, my father lapsed into a private oblivion so deep that he rarely spoke; it was more usual that he would weep.

*

Decades later, when I met Nancy, we compared Jersey shore stories. It was her milieu; I'd visited only on that one occasion. Her beloved hometown of Margate was further south than where Jen and I explored the boardwalk of Seaside Heights. Nancy's house had a porch, a yard. Her descriptions of this idyllic space – playing guitar and singing on the porch with friends, roller-skating down the middle of the street – seemed quintessentially American to me in ways that amused her, as did my lack of familiarity with what to her were basic American things like Cool Whip or KoolAid. I like to picture her on those tarmac roads near the beach, coated in sand: roller-skating, curls deceptively tamed by a 1980s blowout, a smile and a song on her lips.

*

A photo from my parents' engagement party: my mother in a strapless gown that she told me was pale pink, a chiffon skirt flowing from a cinched waist. Her hands are on the table before her and the ring is visible. My father is beside her in a suit, one arm about her shoulders; he is shining with happiness, though likely – I think as I write this – he had also been drinking.

At some point in the weeks prior to that evening, my mother was at home in Sandymount with a cold. My father called to see her and, sitting on the edge of her bed, took from his pocket a felt drawstring bag, spilling its contents onto the bedspread. My mother described looking down in surprise, for what he poured onto her lap were diamonds. She was to choose one for her engagement ring, he said. She laughed telling this story: the ludicrousness of it! Walking from Donnybrook to Sandymount with a pocketful of jewels from his father's business, whistling to himself – my father was a brilliant whistler – perhaps strolling the extra half a road down to the strand to smoke a cigarette and stare across the water before arriving at the front door to chat with my grandmother. And then pouring – pouring diamonds onto the bedspread and my mother and father laughing together at the sight of the starlight glitter. The start of their marriage. They'd called her mother up to see and my grandmother too had laughed at the madness of all of those diamonds – hard but not cold since he'd kept his hand clutched round the bag in his pocket – tumbling through their fingers.

Such theatrical gesture was natural to my father. When I turned eleven – a year during which he was on a national tour of a show and earning a lot of money – he presented me with a birthday card with twenty one-hundred dollar bills inside. It was a huge sum for a child at that time, worth over seven thousand dollars in today's money. I stared at the modest stack with uncertainty; my best friend, there too, urged me to throw the bills into the air and to have them flutter around me while I shouted that I was rich. I couldn't bring myself to do that – so instead Becky duly tossed them, all of us laughing. I gathered the bills soberly enough, though, knowing that the money could and would drop away as in the past, actors' job-to-job existences long familiar to me; I would give them to my mother for the college account that she anxiously fed with all she could spare. But in that moment my father was joyous: generous, excessive, driven by love that he struggled to articulate in the ways that other people did.

Not that I fully understood this at the time; I only knew, as children so sharply do, that I could not rely on him in the same way as I could my mother. He could be here today, on my birthday, with an envelope full of crisp bills, preparing an elaborate meal, helping me with maths homework, and then, tomorrow, in a stupor of vodka and orange juice, a Waterford Crystal glass empty on the floor by the couch with bits of orange pulp glued to its sides.

On those days I let myself into the apartment after school and spent the afternoon in my bedroom. I knew that such descents were more likely after my birthday, after a show's run had ended, when he had a day off; when time opened up before him.

As a pre-teen, I fought him furiously in such states: confronted him, demanded that he stop, poured drinks down the drain. I childishly tried to reason with him, presented what I thought were logical arguments. My mother, much wiser, gently told me that this was a pointless task; addiction had control of him and was beyond logic. But it is difficult for a child to accept their powerlessness. Even when I stopped dumping bottles, I seethed with resentment.

As I closed out high school and headed to college, though, the sympathy for him that had been in abeyance crept back. He no longer drank and had taken a full-time job working in a Madison Avenue wine shop (the announcement of this job leaving my mother open-mouthed). No doubt it helped that I no longer lived at home; I had distance and independence from New York and from my parents.

*

What he wrote about cycling through Belgium offered a glimpse of my father at my own age, only a few years before he met my mother. He wrote so well, presented the images of his trip so clearly. I read the letter in my Trinity Hall room looking out at the Magritte view, seeing my father as not my father but just a boy, really, cycling through a flat, hot European summer, basking in sun, finding swimming pools and rivers in which to cool down. He and his friend practised their French, covered ridiculous distances in a way only fit young people can, stuffed themselves with cream pastries and were surprised to find they loved the bitter black coffee served with a slick of crema that made their breakfast drinks look like tiny Guinnesses.

His companion, who would be his best man, was not at his New York funeral; he was in Ireland, living in the same house he had always lived in on Greystones Main Street. After my father's death he wrote to my mother and asked to see us next time we were both in Ireland. When we met in a small café I stared at him, this man of retirement age who had cycled Belgium with my dad, full of questions. But my mother and he steered the conversation through old times, people and events I was ignorant of. As we waited for the bill I told him about the letter, how my father had described that summer. His face lifted in a smile. We played so much chess, he said.

Chess in Belgium in the sun, he told me, under trees, the sunlight fluttering. It was a small eulogy, one I gathered up gratefully.

*

In the end, I finished the term but cancelled the trip I'd intended to make before Christmas: I needed to get home, to trade the damp cold of Dublin for the freezing dry air of New York. When I got in from the airport, though it was nine days before Christmas, I couldn't stop myself from giving my parents various gifts from relatives back in Ireland, and I couldn't help but give my dad a book I'd bought as part of his present.

There were shadows under my father's eyes that had elongated since September, but he smiled. He wanted to hear all about my classes, what I was reading. We sat there, the three of us, laughing and talking until late. Sleep in, my father said, I have blood tests in the morning and we'll catch up for lunch: though weak, he'd baked baguettes – a preoccupation of decades – and my mother had made soup.

But my jetlag woke me very early, and I walked my parents downstairs to get a taxi to the hospital, waved them goodbye. In memory I am looking at them from my childhood bedroom window, seeing them as small figures all those stories below, stepping into the boxy yellow 1990s taxi and bouncing along the FDR on soft suspension. In fact, though, I was down at street level, having hugged them both before they sat into the cab. Only two hours later, my mother would ring to say that I should come to the hospital, that he was dying.

I thought in later years about the trip I'd planned so carefully – though I'd travelled with my parents and with friends, it was to have been my first time doing so alone, to countries new to me. With no internet, I'd sought out ferry and train timetables from travel agents, and a cousin had sent tickets for the Paris metro with directions to his house. For a year or so I kept the tickets, small slips of paper that held an alternative ending: my father dying in New York while I was on a ferry to Malmo, or on the TGV leaving Paris for Copenhagen. Then, at some point, I let them slip away, put them into a bag of newspapers for recycling, and they became something else.

*

At my father's funeral, I sat with my arm around my mother and the feeling of holding her near is almost all that remains of the service in my mind. Now I wish I had spoken, even though I had little to say. I had never before been to a funeral and didn't know what happened at them, except vaguely – there was a Mass, I understood, but what prayers or rituals were added in I didn't know. I was unaware that family members often spoke. I had no knowledge of burials except for cinematic ones, where people circled a hole in the ground dressed in black, weeping. This seemed unlikely to happen given that my father would be cremated, and also because I had never noticed anything but small historical graveyards in Manhattan.

I remind myself of these things in a bid to let my teenage self off the hook, to excuse the fact that I did not speak: as a middle-aged parent of teenagers, I want the girl I was no longer to feel badly about it, or to feel that it was her responsibility somehow shirked.

The reality was that I could only have said the most generic of things, deployed usual sentiments as a cover for the complexity of feelings that I had. Like a Hallmark card, I would have spoken in powdered-sugar form, or so broadly that it could have been any funeral. I think I could have done that. But to have come up with something truer and kinder to my father himself, to say something that reflected the intense love that he had for me and for my mother, would have been utterly beyond me.

It was an era of overwhelmed feelings and the struggle to articulate them: and also a time of grappling with what I was allowed or able to say. What I had learned from movies was that funerals were for the performance of truisms. But, pushing away from my teens as my father died, I rebelled against this: I wanted to be able to say what I thought was the truth, and if that was unacceptable, or if I did not have the ability to express my feelings with words, I would say nothing, nothing at all.

*

We had found ways to negotiate an inability to speak. Countless times as a child I read lines with him while he was learning or relearning a part – disappearing into *A Midsummer Night's Dream* at the dining-room table, *The Plough and the Stars*, *The Bald Soprano*. If at times in his life he did not know how to talk to me, felt he could share nothing of himself without the risk of breaking down, the necessity of being off-book by the time rehearsals started provided a way of communicating: here was a script we could follow. I was Titania, sometimes Puck, other times Juno or Captain Boyle; I was Nell to his Nagg, or a series of Chekhov characters if he was going into a season of repertory. I read and he performed. The dozens of still photographs used to promote the plays he was in are a reminder of those days when my only role was to cue, occasionally to prompt.

One of the first songs that I learned, aged three (there is a recording), was 'Give My Regards to Broadway'. My father believed there was power in the world of the stage. To inhabit a space dedicated to the ability of mind and language to take us elsewhere, beyond ourselves: this was important to him. Some seasons he spent more time as Joxer or Lear than himself, something that seemed tragic to me when I was entering my teens and at my angriest with him: I was acutely aware that he lived in those performances, that in some ways he felt homeless without a role. As both his body and his performances began to suffer the effects of alcoholism, though, he was offered less theatre work.

He was forced, as I saw it, to be more and more himself, which no doubt initially, though I hope not finally, seemed tragic to him. It was far more complex than what I thought then, of course; he was many and multiple as we all are – there was no pure, refined self that I could have gotten to know even if he hadn't been drinking. When drunk and bereft, he was, perhaps, ever that nine-year-old boy whose mother and sister died so swiftly and for whom he had not known how, or been allowed, to grieve. I have come to believe that we were most ourselves when I played prompter, when we met over words on a page.

*

Among my mother's files I found a notecard my dad addressed to me when I graduated from primary school, aged eleven. In it he said how proud he was, but then, because ours was a household of books and poems and plays, he wrote out, in a hand still instantly recognizable to me, the Yeats poem 'Aedh Wishes for the Cloths of Heaven':

> Had I the heavens' embroidered cloths,
> Enwrought with golden and silver light,
> The blue and the dim and the dark cloths
> Of night and light and the half light,
> I would spread the cloths under your feet:
> But I, being poor, have only my dreams;
> I have spread my dreams under your feet;
> Tread softly because you tread on my dreams.

It is a curious poem to write out for a child, but one that brings tears to my eyes in middle age, understanding as I now do my father's suffering, his sense of failure (wasn't I failing myself?), his desire for things to have been different. I also understand that he did dream for me, in the way that only a disappointed person can, hoping that I would find a way through the mazes that had trapped him; hoping, I see, that I would return to his memory and recall that whatever his failings, he had truly loved and dreamed for me. This small card, decades old, asked my forgiveness, and each time I come across it in a drawer or a folder – released from my mother's files it moves about my house of its own accord – I try to reassure myself that I gave it.

*

For a theatre to go dark was devastating. My father spoke of the spaces of performance with reverence, believing them necessary to our societies: places to pretend and critique, to reimagine of the world. Despite the fact that New York City was never dark, my father left the bathroom light on for me each night when I was small. This was our household version of a ghost light, the solitary bulb that kept a theatre lit after shows had ended and when everyone had departed the building.

Perhaps, after Patsy died, he'd become afraid of the dark. There would have been no small sister down the hall to creep into in the morning for games of marbles on the soft rug; no small sister to walk up the stairs with at night to prepare for bed. He would hardly have understood the room she had occupied in his life, in their family's life, until she was gone. I write the scene. With her curly auburn hair and brown eyes and beaming smile, she'd been full of fun, as he was; she wasn't reserved and cautious like Geddie, the eldest. Patsy had leapt round the garden with him, playing cricket like a mad thing, hardly able to swing the bat upwards for laughing so hard. She'd loved to trick him by sending an apple sailing towards him instead of the ball and *crack!* the apple would shoot apart into smithereens and rain down on the garden. He'd look up in initial dismay at the shower of seeds and flesh and Patsy would be in the grass on her back with the tears already at the corners of her eyes, clutching her tummy. There was the waste of food, the mess of the bat, the particles of apple in their hair: Geddie would give out. But Patsy would hug her round the middle until Geddie softened. Patsy had that effect, and once she was gone the whole house staggered back bewildered as to how to behave.

Who was to throw balls to him, or apples?

Who was to snag at their mother's apron strings singing and dancing as if with a partner while they all enjoyed the sight?

Who was their father to gather on his knee in the evenings by the fire?

The rest of the players were there, ready for their parts, but the central spectacle, the person on whom they trained their collective gaze, was gone.

*

It was not uncommon for children to die then; even cursory glances through census forms from early twentieth-century Ireland reveal litanies of lost lives. And these are the recorded ones. Patsy was from a prosperous home and was well cared for, loved. So many others died anonymously.

When I find her death certificate after much searching, there is a frisson of shock. She did not die in Dublin as I had imagined, close to home; and she was not ten, as I'd thought, which seemed horrendous enough. She was merely six and died in a hospital in Limerick: a place of echoing floors, the bleak grey stonework of the building's front, a place built to save and yet always in a battle with death. Crucifixes, small Marys on painted windowsills, metal bedsteads.

I picture myself sitting at her bedside and stroking her Shirley Temple curls. I see the props of that time: gauze, metal instruments, brown glass bottles, tough woollen blankets. Do I imagine it to be more primitive than it was? It doesn't matter: because however I imagine it she died at six, away from home, away from her brother and sister. It was a Saturday, so perhaps her father, my grandfather, was on his way on the train from Dublin.

Small Patsy, her legs barely making ripples beneath a blanket in the bed; still that young, that unfurled. I sing her a song and hold her soft little hand and I know its size because I have held my children's hands at that age. I know the way that her fingers are still fat with the promise of babyhood and also stronger than one would imagine. Strength in the muscles, yet behind them, barely concealed, bones delicate as birds; tiny things that could so easily be crushed but which daily escape because their owners are wily and fast and lucky. The lashes that rest on her cheeks are brown and shining and curled like my father's, and they do not move: there is not a flutter. I stroke her pale cheeks and tell her that her father is on the way from Dublin and that I'll stay with her until he comes.

I have to stay, because her mother wasn't there. I see the date of death, realizing with horror that her mother had died nine months before. So six-year-old Patsy, going into Barrington's Hospital in Limerick, went almost certainly with an aunt, an uncle, a grandparent, some grown-up who would have left her in and then returned home to other cares, other children, including two not their own, my father and his elder sister.

*

Their mother had died at home on a Friday in February 1938, two weeks after my father's ninth birthday. Had the children – my father – been at school? Had they come back to the house to find the curtains drawn? And their father, had he been at work, or on that last day had he been at home, realizing that his wife and the mother of their three children was breathing her last breaths?

His mother's death on a Friday, Patsy's death on a Saturday.

Did my father's mind forever more think of these losses in relation to the days? I didn't have these facts when he was alive; I never had the chance to ask him.

My own children's births – late Friday into Saturday, and on a blustery sunny Tuesday morning – are forever a part of those days: on a Friday night when the house is dark, the wait for our first baby comes back to me; in a lecture on a Tuesday morning, I cannot but smile thinking of the hasty entrance of our second small boy. When I wake in the middle of the night and cannot fall back asleep, this is what I think of: eyes closed, I go through the labours, the distinctions between them, recalling tiny details. That Donal bought me magazines I never opened on the Friday; that the ward was quiet and dim and that our first born took his time to arrive, allowing us on the other side to pass through to parenthood in slow, sweet enjoyment and desire, as if the thoughtfulness that so defines him was what he began from. That when Donal went out to feed the meter and have a coffee that Tuesday morning several years later, he came back to find me swaying: there was the briefest of walks down the hall, the briefest of discussions about potential pain relief, and then my desperation to explain that there was no more waiting – and our second son, with the exuberant, beaming energy that marks him, was there. He's here, we repeated in amazement to each other. Fridays, Tuesdays: days that made us weep for joy.

For my father, was Friday – gearing up for busy weekends of performance – always the loss of his mother?

Was Saturday – quiet afternoons after my piano lessons, or between shows – the death of Patsy, week in and week out?

After his mother's death: the stilled voices, strange cooking eaten at the familiar table and the pitying glances of all who came and went. Shepherd's pie. Stew. Soda bread. Victoria sponge. Cherry buns. In the cold dim month of the year, neighbours and friends would have dropped in with their offerings of sustenance to the widowed father.

Perhaps Geddie or an aunt or grandmother cosied Patsy on her bed each evening since she was the littlest, and perhaps my father stood aside, full of longing, wanting to climb in as well and avail of the comfort that his twelve-year-old sister and other relatives sought to provide. But he was a boy, *a big help to his father*. Geddie was *a mother to Patsy*; there were new roles for them both. Patsy was the only one not expected to be different, only braver; the one who had never had the chance to come out from behind her mother's skirts. The vanishing act would have been explained several times in the first week:

Will she not come back to me?

She won't, Patsy love; but she will watch over you for the rest of your days.

So Patsy began to have nightmares about this dead mother watching her, hiding in the shadows, and another round of explanation began.

She's not watching over you that way, love, but from heaven.

This paused the nightmares only because it made no sense, like the dreams themselves, and Patsy entered that bewildered grief state on her own, now aware that no one would be able to explain or make clear for her just what had happened.

The death record is a puzzle poem:

Rheumatic
endocarditis
37 years
acute lobar
pneumonia
7 day
Certified

There is no doubt that my father and his two sisters never saw these notations, which are almost all I know of Agnes.

It is much harder to sit at the bed of this dead grandmother; it frightens me to witness her departure from her children.

Would she have been wearing her glasses?

Did she know that she was dying?

Were the children brought to say goodbye?

I don't know.

I stand in the doorway nearly a century after her death and I see her lying there, weakened chest straining to take in breaths, straining to let them out again. Her skin is flat and without any differentiation of pigment from cheek to neck; it is pale and the blood is already deserting her, congealing in her veins. She wears a white flannel nightgown, sensible and warm. It is February; there is a fire in the grate, and hot jars at her feet, but these must be alternated with the cool cloths and air through an opened window, so that when she feels cold she is heated up and then cooled down again savagely when the fever grips her. Her poor body that has birthed and fed three children is now teetering between states, trying so desperately to do what it is meant to do: breathe, breathe, put oxygen into the blood and send it swirling around her body like a rinse.

I put her husband, my grandfather, on the edge of the bed then because she must have someone; there must be someone there to hold her hand and usher her out of the world. Hands are all the difference there is between birthing alone, dying alone. So he sits there in his suit and he weeps; he must weep as he watches his wife cease to be. And he cannot help but think of the children and what will happen to them, but he tells himself not to mind that now. She must ask him for the promise of love for them, mustn't she: I would. I would extract that promise with my last breath.

Tell them I love them. And mind them – mind them for me.

Any words she spoke lost: all of the emotion so strongly felt and lived that goes out like a light, nothing left on in the house.

*

Surprisingly, following a quieting of theatre roles, my father continued to work and stay sober, leaving the house early each morning to meet a colleague for coffee and the companionship of the *New York Times* crossword before the day began.

We didn't know of this routine until his funeral, when the workmate, a single man around the same age, told my mother and I how much he'd appreciated that time with my dad, how much he enjoyed hearing about us. I was surprised at the detail he knew about my mom and I; he told my mother that he only wished he'd heard her sing on stage. He talked about you every morning, he said. With this late friendship, my dad had the opportunity to be a proud father and husband, to express his love for us to someone who knew nothing about his alcoholism and the way in which it had corroded his relationship with us. Sober, ageing and stricken with a cancer that was gradually announcing itself, my father told his friend about my graduation from high school, about my first years in college. He was proud of my brightness, my American-ness, the fact that I was interested in theatre and literature but not in performance. He loved my mother still: her loyalty, goodness, kindness. He hardly spoke of Ireland, except to say that my mother or I were planning to visit or were away.

All of a sudden I saw the father who had been either oblivious in his drinking or overly attentive in his sobriety in companionable quiet over coffee each morning: each man doing the crossword and sharing elements of their lives before they started the work day. I was once more outside my own perspective, the resulting image something unsteady and steady, dependent on multiple points of view.

That half hour of early-morning weekday conversation in an Upper East Side diner stood in contrast to the countless stories I'd absorbed about my father in pubs, theatres, restaurants and hotels that involved many people, much alcohol. Other narratives, other perspectives, were suddenly available; I was young enough that this fell on me with weight, particularly given that the illumination came from a person who, had he not attended the funeral, we would never have known of except vaguely as a colleague. How many people carried such information silently along with them, keeping it to themselves, not ever realizing the value of their insights? This moment marked, in a sense, my starting to think about what a eulogy could be because here, after the official ceremony, my father's friend had handed me a way of proceeding to think of my dad anew.

What sort of eulogy could integrate those various points of view without descending into a series of anecdotes or the recitation of moments? I didn't know. My father's friend might have had more to say, more insight into my father than I had, with my head still turned by teenage concerns. Would a truer eulogy require multiple speakers, a Quaker circle of voices each contributing a vector, or were such attempts vainly searching for a wholeness of person and self that was merely notional? How many people speaking would it take to articulate any human being? Such questions overwhelmed me.

When you're on your own, it's nice to hear about family life, my father's friend told me. We were near the exit of the church where my mother sang in New York. Built in the late sixties after a fire destroyed the nineteenth-century iteration, the church was grey brick with slate floors, rectangular light fixtures and stained-glass windows that shimmered coloured light onto the floors in mirroring columns of twenty, thirty, even forty feet, depending on the angle of the sun. Despite being irreligious, I had always enjoyed spending time in this building, associating it with my mother and her singing. Its difference from traditional churches felt both stylized and austere. I loved the windows, which eschewed complex rosettes in favour of shards of glass fitted together in uncertain ways.

We were standing near a column as my father's friend spoke to us, the colours glowing and fading and glowing and fading like breath, like an irregular heartbeat. It was as if we could all be charged by dancing light. That seemed to me to be the allure of stained glass: the desire to enter into illumination. It was what I had wanted at the Magritte exhibit in September, and what I'd described to my father: the urge to be inside light.

It was, perhaps, why I had bought the exhibit poster and stared into it with such purpose all those months – wanting not the object but its embodiment of experience. The light that the stained glass fired upon the slate floor was the same. I wanted to move beyond the object – the painting, the church – and experience something else, something that reached between people; some state of connection that seemed the realm of adulthood and its relationships, just beyond me. But I also sensed, powerfully, the strangeness of life and the difficulty of knowing anything with certainty, including other people. I felt that I was perhaps too young to understand my own thoughts, my own feelings – and I wanted to seize at the chance to understand. I would have liked to have spoken with my dad's friend for longer; for the day, to try greedily to find out all I could from him, to try to undo my own unknowing. I was at that time prone to these ineffable longings, regularly finding that moments moved on, leaving me with the sense that understanding was always at my fingertips but never in hand.

*

My mother never wanted a grave or a gravestone for herself. I don't want you to feel you have to visit somewhere to think of me, she would say, especially somewhere I've never been that will only be associated with loss. She said this more frequently after my father's death when, as if taken by surprise and unable to think of an alternative, she had purchased a space in a graveyard for him. My father's body was removed from the church and taken off for cremation. A few days afterwards came Christmas, strange and quiet; then after a period the ashes were returned to us in a small urn. My mother, in the meanwhile, had arranged for their burial – the administration and paperwork of death invisible to me then as a teenager.

One day early in the new year, Becky's father drove us out to a cemetery. It was both like and unlike those childhood trips in Becky's family car: familiar to be in the car with someone who, with his wife, Betty, was an old and dear friend. But I remember finding it all very odd; my mother in the front carrying my father's ashes, Chuck driving somewhere outside of Manhattan, everyone talking rather normally until we reached the cemetery. There, as in the movies, as I had tried to picture at the funeral itself, was a hole in the ground, a designated space to contain and control loss, grief, the representation of a person. Someone put the urn into the ground. I think, though I don't remember fully, that a priest was there, and that a few prayers were said, since this would have been part of the ritual. The place, shockingly large, was a maze of gravestones: it was difficult not to consider how much space was given over to the dead. It was also strangely devoid of atmosphere, only solemn and full of small shrubs and fresh flowering plants whose dark compost stood stark against the older brown soil: an awful kind of park. We had not brought plants, but they sold some on site: my mother bought something green; it was January and flowers would not last.

She did not express any interest in visiting the cemetery afterwards. Nor did she actively seek out the graves of her own parents or beloved siblings: once when I took my mother to a spa for a day we passed the graveyard where one of her sisters was buried and she asked to stop but otherwise never visited such monuments. For a person of faith she had a peculiar, individual approach to these conventions.

After her death, I wondered about having my father's ashes brought back to Ireland. But I had no idea where the cemetery with my father's ashes was. I pictured visiting and extracting a handful of soil to return home with, something to add to the earth surrounding the cherry tree we planted in the Wicklow garden and where we placed my mother's ashes. I haven't done that.

As my oldest son closes in on the age that I was when my father died, I have an acute awareness of the distance between us, the gap in time since I was at his deathbed, at the cemetery: lifetimes ago. And sometimes, in passing the Magritte poster, more than thirty years old, now framed and on a wall in my home, I wish it could function for me as a portal and not only a view.

BIRTH STORIES

The drive at dawn was terrifying, only weeks into our experience as parents; Donal and I didn't speak except to the baby, who was so fevered as to be inconsolable. He cried in unfamiliar mewling sounds that seemed to my frantic mind to be diminishing; he was sinking into listlessness. There was no traffic at that hour, but it felt like we had never lived so remotely, never been so far from a hospital. I sat in the back beside the baby's car seat, trying not to touch him because I was so afraid of adding to the heat of his tiny body – yet all I wanted was to hold him. Donal drove grim-faced, clocking mile after mile on the motorway, trying to eye the baby in the rear-view mirror.

Nothing prepared me for the true shock of parenthood: not the fabled sleepless nights or the fatigue that cloaks life and keeps it at a distance, but the density of the love, accompanied by a new and wondrous kind of worry.

You learn to live with that worry. It doesn't go away, merely transmutes as a child passes from stage to stage. But on that drive, on that morning, Donal and I were afraid as we'd never before been about anything. Our world narrowed, peripheralities disappearing as in a cartoon as our attention zeroed in on this particular human that we called ours.

We were whirled, the baby was whirled, out of our arms and onto an examination table, where electrodes and sticky wires began to proliferate on his small chest and ribcage. I became so distressed by his hoarse screams as needles probed miniscule veins that a doctor told me I would have to leave if I couldn't stop crying. The threat of separation shocked me into silence and I stood at his head, my hands cupping his face, whispering reassurances into his ears.

The unreal quality of that hour: manic movement around our baby, the setting up of an intravenous line, the rapid beginning of antibiotic treatment and delivery of vast amounts of Calpol to bring his fever down while they tested blood samples. And then the strange quietening as his fever dropped and the antibiotics began to overwhelm what was, in the end, an easily treatable infection. The activity lessened, the baby slept; Donal and I stood looking at each other wide-eyed.

In the immediate aftermath, during moments when my breath was ragged as if I'd run at breakneck pace, I wondered how my father's father had coped ever again after the loss of Patsy: I had that conscious thought, the dread still tremoring through me.

Several days later we were still in hospital, but the baby was recovering with intravenous antibiotics, being monitored closely. We would be allowed home soon. In the meanwhile bodily exhaustion battled my continuing need to be there, to be with the baby every hour of the day. A hospital vomiting bug dried up my milk in hours. I cried until I had the thought that the tears wasted fluid my body needed for milk production, and then, under duress – Donal and a nurse insisting – I was sent up to the rooms that parents could rent by the night, told to sleep in a proper bed for the first time since we'd entered the hospital.

It was a hotel of the condemned; no one wished to stay in these rooms. Because if you were trying to put yourself to sleep here it meant a child was ill, that something was wrong enough to warrant the need to be in the building; it meant that you were afraid to go home. When we arrived I had refused these rooms upstairs, though, which felt too far away; until becoming sick myself I had stayed instead on a kind of yoga mat on the floor of our baby's room. Each evening someone came around and delivered to me and other parents or relatives mats and piles of white sheets, a blanket, a white pillow in a starched case.

I sat in a vinyl hospital chair holding and feeding the baby. Eventually, I would put him into the cot and hope that he would sleep for a few hours. Then I lay down on the mat beside him and tried to find rest amid the hospital sounds, raising myself often to peep into the cot. It was unnatural to be away from Donal, who each evening left late to get some rest before having to return to work in the morning. It felt wrong too to be below the baby's sleeping level, to be unable to feel him next to me. And so, like the baby, I dozed, jolted awake, dozed again.

The ward was mostly quiet, because there were only a dozen or so individual rooms for quite seriously ill children, or – in our case – for newborns, whose illnesses were taken seriously. Not long into our admission we'd known that our child was okay, that he could be quickly cured of this infection, and he returned to his placid self: worn out, but fine. And the gratitude we felt, so powerful that it swept through our own bodies like those antibiotics, that gratitude was underwritten by the terror we'd experienced and which was echoed everywhere in the building. You shake afterwards, realizing safety.

The nap upstairs in the dark room – I remember greens and browns and a comfortable bed, but no details – allowed me to recover. I stopped throwing up. When I woke, showered and went downstairs, Donal was sitting in the vinyl chair, the baby against his chest, both of them dozing. My milk returned and I could shed tears again.

The last day in hospital, rid of the vomiting bug, sitting there holding our contented baby and knowing that Donal would be collecting us, I felt, finally, a version of relaxed. There had been a television in the room the whole week, but I only turned it on that day, when it felt I no longer had to be on high alert. We didn't have a television at home and so it was a novelty, like watching movies on planes. The baby fast asleep in my arms, I became engrossed in the film version of *Touching the*

Void. A serious mountain climb goes wrong: conditions deteriorate and one climber ends up holding the rope of the other, who has plummeted over a crevasse in snow-blind conditions. Getting no response on the rope, the first climber chooses to cut it in an attempt to save himself. In still terrible conditions, he manages to make his way back to base, where he informs a waiting person of what has happened. They hold a makeshift ceremony, burning the second climber's clothes, and are preparing to leave when the second climber crawls, broken, over unimaginably challenging terrain, having survived the unthinkable.

I told Donal about it when he came in. Our family was yet to become obsessed with climbing, so the story had no resonance for me in that way, but we – like everyone else who read the book or saw the film, I imagine – considered the choice that the first climber made. Was it right? Would we have done the same? The story had so much in it – survival against odds, questions of trust and responsibilities – that holding our warm baby I kept imagining the scene: the first climber sitting there, heels dug into packed snow, connected to a climbing partner he could no longer see or hear, only feel the weight of through the rope in his hands. The extreme tension of that fibrous anchor.

*

At the end of the ward was a tiny communal kitchen that had several chairs, a small refrigerator, a kettle. Families from all over Ireland came to this hospital. There were grandparents down from Sligo since their grandson's parents had to work and mind other children. The grandfather, eating ham sandwiches and drinking mugs of tea, told me about his grandson's acid reflux. It was so severe the child had been disappearing before their eyes. The baby, about six months' old now, slept on a steeply inclined pillow. He was gaining weight again as doctors worked their way through a battery of allergy tests, feeding him intravenously so that his wee oesophagus could heal. Arms are pincushions, the grandfather said, and he shoved heavy spectacles against the bridge of his nose to deal with the emotion of it. He'd never spent much time in Dublin before, he told me, and this experience only made him hanker for home: he wasn't going until the small boy was ready to come too.

In addition to the grandfather of the reflux baby, there was a nervous young woman drinking dark tea who had children in the hospital on two different wards. She pressed the mug between her palms, holding it against her breastbone as if for the comfort of warmth, and nodded at me in greeting.

Did you see about the petrol bomb thrown into the front windows of the house out West? That's her kids, the grandfather said plainly. Both burned to bits.

I had seen the news and couldn't hide my horror.

My daughter's pajamas melted into her skin, the woman told me, jiggling one leg over the other. Don't know what life'll be like for her or for her sister. She was dry-eyed. And they won't catch the feckers, I know they won't. Already done a runner to Matagorda I bet they have.

When her tea was finished she excused herself to nip outside for a cigarette, something she did a set number of times a day and only if her children were both sleeping. She hated the idea that they'd wake and panic if she wasn't there.

We shared biscuits, milk for tea and coffee. The grandfather accepted an apple, once, and then sat eating it with determination, this variation in his watchman's diet. Someone might leave a box of chocolates on the small table alongside an ever-present box of tissues.

Another child, in the next room to ours, was dying of cancer. As they'd wheeled our baby from the emergency room to the ward, the mother sobbed in the hallway on the payphone (for this was in the early days of mobiles, and people were forced to have private conversations in public spaces). She was speaking to her father. Daddy, she wailed, Daddy, they say there isn't any more treatment. We were mortified to have to walk through this conversation.

The nurse wheeling our baby squeezed the woman's upper arm, then gently touched her neck before returning her hand to the trolley. Did the woman feel the weight of the nurse's hand?

At night that baby, who was perhaps nine months or a year – I was too new a parent to judge – cried when his soother popped out of his mouth. The nurses were always on call, never sleeping; their swiftness and tirelessness amazed me. But one time when he cried they were all tending to other children, and I couldn't bear it. Hesitating, because I felt like I was doing something wrong, I went in to his room and replaced the soother. He stopped crying immediately and looked at me for a moment – as in the theatre, it is never truly dark in hospitals – before closing his eyes again. He was so much sturdier and solid looking than our newborn in the room next door; I couldn't fathom that he could be ill, that something beneath the soft skin and downy hair was wreaking havoc, invisibly pulling him away from his existence.

We left the hospital with a gurgling baby in tow. I controlled my impulse to weep for joy because many families went home without their child, walked through that exit alone, and I knew I had no right to cry.

*

When I can't sleep and I think of our children being born, my remembrances are not narratives and they are not rituals, but they are prayerful. My mother taught me prayers as a child and liked to recite them with me when I was very small, and while I never believed, I loved the closeness of the time with her. Instead of teaching our own children prayers, we read to them and told them stories, and on occasion when they were small and needed the reassurance of hearing what joy their arrivals had created, I told them about their birthdays: details about our preparations at home, the weather on those particular days, about their tiny clothes.

But I don't know that I could write of these experiences, not as broad, life-changing events, in any case. I don't remember them start to finish; they are not clear and whole in my mind. Instead, there are specific, fragmented memories that flash inside me sometimes, that go off like bodily fireworks and remind me: my God! I have grown babies! and, with Donal, have delivered them day by day and year by year through the world.

Sometimes I find myself astonished to look back and realize – we managed to feed them, mind them, prepare their food, wash their clothes, bathe them, drive them to school, sing them to sleep with repeating rounds of 'Puff the Magic Dragon' or 'Jingle Bells' or 'Hush Little Baby'. We hoisted and carried them, held them when they fell or cried or simply wanted to be held, built Lego extravaganzas, impersonated stuffed toys and dolls' voices, baked with them, read with them, played games that came and went.

We collected wet autumn leaves and summer daisies, pebbles and sticks and shells and driftwood and siftings of sand, emptied these things from tiny pockets into bowls because they were precious. We kicked and threw and caught and hit balls of all sizes and shapes, often retrieving them from hedges and fields, returning triumphant and bramble-scratched. We bundled small tired bodies into car seats after swims and watched as drowsiness overtook them like a coming wave, drove an extra mile to let them sleep, idling the car in the driveway for the quiet, the extra minutes, then gently tugged and pulled off seat belts and carried them, sleep-heavy, up to the house.

In the dark night of winter and the neverdark of summer I fed them from breasts that were full and sometimes wholly emptied. For thousands of nights we slept with small hands holding on to us some which way – our hair, ears, noses, nipples all providing the surety that we were there, that they were safe. For thousands upon thousands of days, we did these things.

The enormity of the task can't be surmised in those initial moments after birth, when we stared with simple amazement and tenderness at our children, at each other. And then one day, quite suddenly, we realize that it has been years since a child has crawled into our bed, years since my breasts hurt with the emptiness of constant feeding, years since we have had to carry one of our children, that out of those thousands of times of picking them up, one – only one – was the last.

*

So overjoyed I could not cry or do anything except gush thanks inarticulately after our first baby was born, not two years later I lay on the floor of the bathroom in the immediate aftermath of a late miscarriage that left me in tatters. I knew that it, or some ending like it, was coming; it had been a long, heartbreaking Saturday. After I'd started bleeding, my brother-in-law drove me into hospital and my in-laws stepped in to mind C, since Donal was on a film set and couldn't get away. After hours of waiting – the anxiety of the room full of pregnant people, everyone wide-eyed, afraid to talk in case their fears were realized in that awful space, in case someone else's heartbreak was contagious – I was scanned.

In my memory there was none of the usual chat as my lower belly was smeared with lube; in my memory it was as if no one was there in the room. The machine told me with its dispassionate silence, its lack of throb, there was no heartbeat. But then the people who were there all along asked me if I was sure of my dates, because the size of the foetus didn't match what I was telling them; from the start, I thought now, something had been wrong. Our doctor wasn't on call and there was no one to perform a D&C until Monday; I had to leave knowing that the not-yet-baby was dead.

Because phones can't ring on a film set even on such occasions, I found myself texting Donal, worrying about him worrying about me, trying to reassure him. My brother-in-law drove me back home, where I made C dinner and put him to bed, lying with him to read book after book, nursing him to sleep, trying to focus on what was in front of me, on what I had to be grateful for. I had this beautiful child lying beside me; I had milk for him; I had his clinging hand on my collarbone.

Trying not to think that a part of me was literally dead. Trying not to wonder how this had happened.

C drifted off and I watched his face, the slight tremblings of his eyelids as dreamsleep overcame him, milk on his breath. Eventually, as noiselessly as possible, I crept from the bed and sat vacantly at the kitchen table. I'd lost my bearings, felt I'd forgotten to do something crucial.

And then labour started – though I didn't recognize it immediately. I was in such anguish that the physical pain didn't register: only as it worsened and I texted Donal did it begin to dawn on me, the pain coming from far away in my mind to rest in my lower back and belly. I writhed silently on the floor of the bathroom, not wanting to risk C toddling in. Donal was finally on his way home. I had been bleeding heavily for a few hours at that point, and when he saw me he rang the hospital straightaway. Since they advised coming in, once again my brother-in-law was called upon, this time to stay in the house with C. I was frightened at that stage. I knew that the foetus was dead, there was no hope. But it hadn't occurred to me to be concerned about myself until the bleeding went on and on and on and I felt weak, shaky, not myself. My thinking was grainy, turning back and back again on C, on not wanting to leave him motherless: I was thinking of my father, just turned nine, attending his mother's funeral. My pulse was uneven, my heart thudding in my throat as if trying to speak for me.

But by the time my brother-in-law arrived it was over; the contractions had progressed to breaking point and I finally miscarried on my own in the bathroom. I could feel it: the suddenness and physical solidity of tissue passing out of me, falling away from my body. I collapsed on the toilet for long moments, my head towards my feet, my arms hanging dead-weight. Then I sank to the floor and lay there. The exhaustion, the sense of being rent, was total. Donal was calling anxiously through the door. Hesitating and in a kind of shock, standing like a colt on jellied legs, I flushed the toilet. The contractions stopped – which is when I suddenly realized they had been contractions – and, leaning on Donal, I hobbled out, still thinking we would have to go to hospital. We got in the car, drove in November dark the short distance uphill where a spine of road overlooks the Glendalough valley. There, at the entrance to a forest, I asked Donal to pull in. In my memory we could see the aurora borealis, green swirls of lights in the sky. We had seen this spectacle there before, just once: we'd gone up on the hill very late when it had been in the news that the lights might be visible in Ireland. But it wasn't that night. The fact that my memory tries – every time – to insert something cosmic into that moment says it all: something in my own tiny universe had changed. I felt – I knew – that it was over. My body was quiet. The bleeding was tapering. We turned the car around, having driven only that one kilometre. The night was, in memory, cold, with sharp shards of stars over the hills on the way back down. I crawled back into bed and stayed there, empty. My brother-in-law remained in the house just in case we suddenly needed to depart, but the rest of the night was uneventful. I was too shocked for much sleep. Donal tried to comfort me without speaking, since there were no words to say. When C slid over the side of the cot as usual around 6 am, he came into our bed and fed for the last time; he never sought milk from me again, as if the night's experience had so marked my breast milk that he decided he had had enough. Rather than out the windows, which we were still dark at that hour, I stared at the Magritte poster that morning, aware of another shift in perspective, of it being lodged in my body.

*

For years – so many now – I think of flushing the toilet, the anguish that moment cost me. There is the wishing that the miscarriage had not happened, yes, but also the persistent wondering if I should have retrieved the remains from the violent red of the toilet bowl. I have imagined what it might have felt like, to lift something so soft and unformed, to have examined my body's terrible failure, to have stared at that impossible future. Perhaps the reality of it would have been easier than this imagining, year by year by year, decade by decade.

Occasionally if we mention the possibility of moving, consider life carrying on elsewhere, I think of two things: my mother's ashes in the soil of a particular cherry tree visible from the kitchen windows, and the remains of our not-yet-baby somewhere in the ground beneath me.

*

Thankfully no one uttered the platitude that I was lucky to have a living child. (I knew I was lucky.) But the absence of my child's sibling – for months it strangled me.

It was impossible, once on that track of pregnancy, not to think in terms of what week or month it was. Early spring was hardest, because there was a due date to cope with. On that day I allowed myself to imagine a different labour from the one I had undergone. C, at eighteen months a fluent and adroit talker, knew that something was wrong. He carried me teddies, stuffing them into my arms for hugs; he stuffed himself into my arms. I'd kept a scan, slick-papered from the sonographer's machine, of the foetus from when its heart still beat. When C found the image in the back of a notebook I was writing in

I explained. His sister, he called it. And with the blunt compassion of small children, he comforted me by telling me that he would have loved that baby, too, that he too missed and loved that baby.

It mattered to me a great deal, that picture, the proof of the life I'd imagined. It was evidence, something to say that I had not *merely* imagined, but had also physically conceived of this life. But like many things we cherish when we grieve, it slipped away as the grief limited itself to sharp assaults instead of constant ones. Now I don't know in what notebook it might be contained, or whether it has disappeared for good.

*

Donal and I married two months after losing the baby, when I should still have been pregnant. I have a distinct memory from school of two friends who were sisters describing how they would promenade down the aisle when they were grown up; I was bemused at the allure of such a ceremony and knew that I would dread people looking at me in such a moment. I'd never been interested in marriage; never, as a young girl, imagined wedding dresses or ceremonies. What mattered was the state of the relationship Donal and I were in, and not any legal definition of it. We had survived thunderstorm summers as students in Munich, made it through several years of long-distance letter-writing, eventually made a home together in first Dublin and then Wicklow – and despite buying a house, creating a garden and having one child together, we had never considered getting married. The house, the garden, the child: these *were* marriage.

But friends casually told us one evening that under Irish law, someone could potentially challenge Donal for guardianship of our children were something to happen to me. With the passionate, hormonal anxiety of the pregnant, I fretted. Together we imagined my death and the worst-case scenario of someone attempting to take C and this new baby away from him. It was unbearable. There was no one – not a single real person – we could imagine challenging Donal in that way, but we decided to marry before the baby was born.

The decision was not merely dispassionate; the reality was that the love Donal and I have has been the totalising narrative of my life: something uncontainable in fragments. He was the reason I'd made the reverse migration of my parents, coming 'home', as my mother put it. The idea that, were I to die, this man whom I loved above any person on the planet, who was the gentlest, kindest, most loving and madcap parent any child could wish for, that he could be prevented from being with our children? It made me wild. While for almost fifteen years nothing had occurred to make me feel that marriage would change the way that we existed together, now, baby in belly, C clambering over us, I found myself suddenly afraid not to be married.

We planned to marry with only C and the not-yet-baby present. We had rings engraved with a quotation from Michael Ondaatje's work, the only author we wholeheartedly agreed on: *The heart is an organ of fire* in minute script around the outside of the bands. When our January wedding day arrived, sharply cold and more like New

York than Irish winter, there were only the three of us, after all. A woman married us, another woman from the registry was our witness, and C sat on our laps. Is this the day we are getting married? he asked. And it was the three of us who got married, taking a few pictures ourselves, chilled to bone by a migraine-bright wind.

The day was underwritten by the loss of the baby that had prompted the wedding. The legal bond now signalled another: the feat of surviving grief's initial onslaught, of putting in day after day, moving into a new future that was distinct from that imagined one and also, indelibly, marked by it.

*

I was so traumatized by my miscarriage that it almost destroyed our (new) marriage. Grieving for what no one could see, I wanted desperately – desperately – to be pregnant again. I could imagine nothing else that would allow me to heal. And Donal, traumatized himself and struggling to cope with my enormous feelings, decided that the last thing that he wanted was to try to have another baby.

The rage I felt was white-hot. It was.

I tended not to speak of the trauma of that day, though I still recalled the shock of the first sign of blood and was revisited by the eventual rupture within me. I told friends what had happened (though without detail), and of course Donal and I spoke of it. But I wanted to speak of it more. More than was acceptable, really; more than anyone was prepared to listen. My feelings were torrential; I felt excessive. This was embarrassing for people. There was a too-muchness about my emotions, which were grounded in my body. In a queue while grocery shopping I would hear the squall of a small baby. Immediately my breasts would swell with unneeded milk and I'd have to battle through the urge to pick C up and run away from the sound. I didn't want to meet friends for a walk or coffee and narrate again what had happened (though I sometimes couldn't help myself). I didn't want to spend evenings after we'd put C to bed reliving the loss with Donal (though I did this too): especially since this often, inevitably, led to another row about what I wanted, what he didn't.

And so I stopped speaking of it aloud. Instead I leaned heavily on an online pregnancy loss forum and daily typed my grief. There were a half-dozen of us who became regulars; all of us had endured recent, even multiple, losses; two had lost babies at full term, and one, tragically, at one month. We were different ages and from different locations, unlikely to have met or to have become friends in other circumstances, but we became a lifeline for each other, marking milestones that might have been, buoying each other up as due dates came and went, as attempts to get pregnant failed – or as attempts to get pregnant were successful and terror set in.

Gradually we shared details of our day-to-day lives and eventually met in person, remaining in touch for years afterwards; I still think of them and remember their babies. Each of us found that life did not quite afford a space to mourn; the too-muchness of our grief, the awkward voluptuousness of it, scared people. Few wanted to see our lunar landscape scan images, to see photographs of our babies with lips darkened by death. To those who had not experienced such losses, these things were macabre. They sent people flying for cover, afraid, as we humans so often are, of contagion.

In the event, though, you cling to pieces of evidence of what you have loved, these signs of what you have lost. We shared these things with each other. There was no explanation needed, no apology for being awkward or too excessive in our feeling. Almost always someone was having a day marked by the struggle simply to get out the door, and almost always one of us was having a better day and could offer comfort.

In retrospect, you look back and wonder. How did those days pass?

In the same way that you realize you have not been required to unclip a child's seatbelt, or get them dressed, you realize that today you have not wept.

*

I came to accept that I would have no more children, knowing that my fortune lay in what I had with Donal and C. But Donal, it turned out, changed his mind. Several years later I gazed at O, in the hospital in the blue light of night time, alone with him for the first time. What I felt was fervent, sublime thankfulness. It returns when I see my boys hug their father, when they hug me, when Donal and I catch eyes: something in defiant contrast to life's heartbreak, my love and gratitude something sensed in the viscera.

When she arrived from New York to meet O, my mother, who had struggled to conceive, who had privately worried she was dying of cancer when she was actually, finally pregnant; my mother who had cried with me on the phone after our miscarriage, sat with tear-sparkled eyes with our new baby against her shoulder. I can't believe you have another child, she said to me.

And I barely replied, because I couldn't believe it either.

OBJECT MEMORY

In the months and years following my father's death my mother readjusted her life once more. She had done this on leaving Ireland, on leaving Arizona, then Seattle; on arriving in New York; on having a child; on leaving the theatre for a desk job. After my dad died I had returned nervously to college in Ireland, worried about her being on her own in New York. But for the first time in her life, she had a space totally her own. She joined a book group and auditioned for a second choir. Not long afterwards she retired early.

The long letters she wrote to me were vivid: she began her days with Barry's Tea and knitting on the white sofa she bought herself for the apartment; she sat each morning looking out at the river from several dozen floors up, watching seaplanes and helicopters, ferries and tugs. Favourite books of poetry, some in Irish with English translations on the facing pages, lay on her coffee table.

She read *The New York Times* each morning, too, picking it up from outside her door after her first cup of tea. She included clippings from the paper; she knew that I missed the hard copy and carefully preserved book reviews, film reviews (for Donal), recipes, articles that struck her in particular ways or that she read with an eye on history (an early write-up on Obama; the entire paper the day after 9/11).

The letters were a lively patter of what she was singing and reading, what show or exhibit she had seen, what opera was next in the season. Her writing was full of gratitude: for the dimension of sky she saw from her eyrie, for the good friends with whom she had such fun, for the life that she found herself in.

Over the next fifteen years my mother visited chateaux in France and drove around Italy with friends. She sang in Austria, Germany, Russia and China, took a jaunt to England with her eldest sister, and visited us several times a year. Every time she arrived with gifts from her travels or from New York: a turquoise Murano glass vase that she carried in bubble wrap by ferry, car and plane; a hand-painted French serving platter; nesting dolls from Russia; silk from China. Her last major trip was to Australia, Tasmania and New Zealand, aged seventy-six.

But there were signs of her mind beginning to falter. She arrived for a holiday in Ireland with one suitcase full of presents for our son, her first grandchild, but another was filled with random things including yards of something Donal and I thought might be garden netting – but no clothes. She became terrified when she received credit card statements that said she owed nothing, because she had begun to think that these were bank statement balances and that all of her money had disappeared. She called in distress because the thought of cooking dinner for two old friends for Thanksgiving was overwhelming. We solved many of the problems through phone calls, but I was increasingly resorting to ringing New York friends, hers and mine, to step in. There was a growing sense of the impossibility of the distance, a push to arrange her long-cherished aim of returning to Ireland.

Then came a call from New York to tell me that she'd collapsed while walking to a choir rehearsal and had been taken to hospital. They ran a brain scan that afternoon and wanted to perform further tests. My mother refused and told me jubilantly that she had climbed out the window of her room, something I assume was untrue in a city obsessed with window guards at any height. What is true is that she left behind in the hospital her coat and house keys, simply going to her neighbour and dear friend Joann for the spare set; Joann's phone call to me was the first I heard of what had happened.

My mother told me that she was fine. She had been exhausted with all of the extra singing for Easter services. There'd been no need for the brain scan; she'd wanted to get home to her own bed. She sounded normal, chatted to the children and heard C's stories and news, asked toddling O questions that he listened to with great seriousness and answered with yeses and nos, smiling. I hovered uneasily nearby, wondering what to do. Hurry over and fly her back with me earlier than planned? She was adamant: she wasn't ready to leave. She was going to walk to the farmers' market with Joann as usual. They would sit to have coffee somewhere, or a slice of pizza, or a bagel; she didn't know what they'd feel like. The cherry blossom was out in Stuyvesant town and around Gramercy Park and they'd walk that way to enjoy the day.

*

We paid a small fortune to ship my mother's things to Ireland from New York, but in the time that it took these items to arrive – the winter weeks the boat crossed the Atlantic, darkly moving – her desire for them slipped away. Gradually, externalities had ceased to matter. When I told her that the shipment had safely arrived, she said, oh I don't need any of that. A truck nonetheless drove her belongings to my home, and we piled boxes in the room we called the study. One or two contained things of my own, books from childhood, old letters, my dollhouse contents; the rest were my mother's, a few legacies of my father's.

For a few days I wandered into the room and looked at the stacks of cardboard boxes, marvelling at the way they contained multiple pasts – and also at my mother's disinterest. Unopened, they were furniture-like and regular, uniformly the tawny gold of cardboard, but they made me anxious. They were not furniture; they had no use, and each time I found myself peeling back a strip of tape, peering into arrays of objects sadly out of place.

I tried to tempt my mother into the study with what I found, bringing her a favourite knick-knack or book to hold in her hands with their riverine veins. Her responses were similar to how she reacted to my children (and surely to me as well decades earlier) when they brought her some special toy or book to examine. She exclaimed over what I handed her, admired it to please me, sometimes even provided a narrative – she'd had the Plácido Domingo memoir signed at the Met Book Shop, had been presented the case for holding knitting needles by a brilliant seamstress friend she'd met at their Shakespeare class for retirees – but then put it aside with a gentle pat or a quiet gesture, as if she didn't want to offend me.

As a result it was myself and the children who decorated her new apartment in Dublin, positioned sofa and chairs, placed the photo albums on a coffee table; Donal hung her paintings, shelved books. The children arranged her music next to a CD player, tested the toaster. We structured a set, built scenes in which we hoped that she would be able to continue to live her life. On a new sideboard we placed a heavy crystal bowl of polished stones, crystals and minerals, which she'd collected over the years from Astro Gallery in New York. The gallery was near a bus stop she frequented, and if it was raining she went in to gaze at the meteorites and refrigerator-sized crystals, buying miniatures that settled neatly in the palm, at first because she was conscious of using the store as an umbrella and then because the weight of them in her hand was so lovely.

Amid the purchased things were a select scattering of stones and shells from beaches, mostly in Ireland, but also a few from her travels: a bit of gleaming paua from New Zealand, a razor-clam shell from Tasmania, some bay scallops from the Jersey shore, smooth pebbles from the edge of the Yangtze before the flooding for the Three Gorges Dam, and a very old piece of coral that someone had given her in Hawaii half a century earlier, before, she always added, people had stopped snapping off portions of reefs as souvenirs and started destroying them in other ways.

But even this slowly built collection no longer mattered to her. Each time we visited she tried to give it away. The children were offered, and accepted, the shimmering bowl, carrying it away like an orb of light between them. They were delighted, having played with the stones and shells and crystals through the years in New York; they sorted, claimed favourites, invented games.

My mother urged me to take home the once-treasured Yale Shakespeare set, many of the blue cloth-bound volumes filled with my parents' notes for parts they played over decades on stage. But I didn't want to accept the books, because to do so was to acknowledge to her that something was pending, that we were proximate to death. My mother, though, did not struggle against that ending: she parsed her present with a boldness that sometimes frightened me. I was already aware that time was running out in that newly decorated apartment, in a sheltered housing scheme. When we knelt to dig in lavender and primroses outside her front door in the sun, I was already wondering how many years of bloom we'd see.

*

While my mother tried to rid herself of objects, we were accumulating them. I was amazed to find our house a dynamic and shifting space of things, many of which were lethal underfoot. When our second child was born, Donal's father joked, as he and Donal's mum arrived with bags of presents, that now we were really gished: our home was about to be filled with plastic junk. Sometimes it felt as though we were permanently stooped to collect blocks, dominoes, elements of marble runs, squeaky toys, stacking toys, musical instruments, teddies, small dolls and their clothes, play doctor's equipment.

Playdough in lurid colours dried hard and had an aroma faintly reminiscent of my own childhood. Glittering putty left on a table eventually spread its way to the edge, dripping onto carpet, or was flung into a toy basket where it sludged into every crevice, settling into the fur of favourite teddies, the hair of beloved dolls. When small hands became dextrous enough for scissors and limbs long enough to open every door in the house, we might enter a bathroom to find snippings of toilet paper in heaps – accompanied, alarmingly, by tufts of hair.

We tried to stay on top of the detritus, avoiding the plastic crap Donal's dad warned about when we could, buying from second-hand shops and regularly passing on our own outgrown toys and clothes. But still there were mounds of objects and strange shrines about the house. Windowsills became staging grounds for dominoes or an impromptu arts-and-crafts session; the kitchen table was rarely free of games and projects.

For a time we lived with glitter permanently dusting our hair; for another we lived with potions in various states of decay and propagation, fuchsia flowers, daisy petals, blades of grass, sprigs of herbs from the garden swilling in any container the children could get their hands on. My mother's shimmering stones were ranged on desks and shelves; dozens of favourite books tiled the living-room floor, the kitchen, bedrooms. You could walk into a room and find a horde of stuffed creatures in the middle of a school lesson run by one or other child. Or – as happened often if I remained in the kitchen cooking or working while they played with friends – you could enter the hallway to find it completely blocked with cushions from every sofa and chair in the house, a barricade eight foot tall over which were fired dozens of foam bullets.

The children's inventiveness meant that objects did not remain in place, were not fixed in their minds as they were in mine: even large furniture was not immoveable. They imposed themselves on their environments in ways that continuously surprised me: it was disconcertingly sad to arrive into a sitting room in which couches had been stripped so thoroughly that the only seating available was – tentatively – on springs, the floor almost entirely covered in random objects. It reminded me of college parties, the raucous destruction – rooms looked as if they themselves were drunk.

And then the children's friends would go home or it would near dinner time and together, small hands and larger ones, we would begin the daily task of putting the house back together. Sometimes in the evening after they were asleep I would sit and find that in the same way your ears ring after much noise and conversation, my eyes vibrated from the sight of the many things, brightly coloured and strangely shaped, that had passed through my hands through the day, among them usually some of my mother's.

*

It is easy to look back and think of the things that I had to do when my mother moved home to Ireland: a lot of driving to visit and collect her to stay with us at weekends; laundry; shopping; increasing numbers of medical appointments; endless paperwork to transfer her life from New York back to Ireland. Rather than the objects she tried to gift to me, I took on tasks.

I'd receive panicked phone calls from my mother: about her bank card, the toaster, a door lock. These objects no longer worked because her mind puzzled over their function. How did the card amount to money? The washing machine became as complex as a space shuttle, buttons and programs and dials that she stared at without recognition. Crying, she autodialled my number, following simple instructions taped in large writing to the phone.

There was a fine drama when she returned to her apartment with the wrong clothes, and another resident, also losing cognitive function, accused her of having an affair with her elderly, declining boyfriend: how else had his clothes turned up in my mother's room? He had no way of explaining, either. Panicked phone calls came too from the manager of the sheltered housing scheme to say my mother had gone missing again. She would go out for long walks and not return, lost in her attempts to find the familiar ground that was a continent away, or in an Ireland a half-century gone. I once had a call from the guards, who picked her up when it became apparent she had walked herself along the seafront into exhaustion and a confusion so thorough that she was seeking a yellow cab for a ride back to her apartment in New York. In her bag they'd found the wallet from which I had deliberately removed cards: it contained cash, my phone number and the items she'd placed there herself through the years: photos of me as a child, photos of Donal and I, photos of my children, a business-card-size version of a prayer someone had given her that was worn to softness, some saint figured in black ink. A medal the size of a pinkie nail with a sliver of blue satin ribbon was also tucked into a wallet pocket, an embossed figure that might have been Mary, a protective talisman.

The first year of my mother's return was a blur of caring responsibilities packed in around work and children. At the end of each week I now collected her, her laundry, whatever items were causing trouble (we tried several kettles) and she came home to us, where my children's delight in her presence began to totter towards confusion at her behaviour.

When Donal and the kids and I managed a weekend back in Mayo at the end of the first year, I curled into a ball on the bed sobbing after a run along the coast, unable to do anything but cry. I could barely think, let alone write. And yet the toll it was taking on me was nothing compared to the impact on her. At eighty, my mother was trying to map a new environment just as her cognition was beginning to fail.

I'd tried to organize her Dublin apartment to mimic the layout of her New York space, placing the bed in the same position with regards to the door, for instance. Countless afternoons she and I practised walking to the small shop near her new place; we went to the bus stop and took rides to the seafront, which was more familiar. As we walked we talked in detail about what we saw. This was my amateur way of trying to register a pattern of landmarks in her mind: particular trees, a letter box on a corner, the name on a house.

We spoke together, my failing mother and I, about space and location and geography in the way that parents speak with their children to map their worlds – the way my mother had spoken with me, and the way that the ancients practised remembrance through the creation of metaphysical maps based on the physical world.

But the rehearsals were no use. After nearly fifty years in New York she'd woken in the Dublin suburbs. Ireland had changed drastically, and so, of course, had she. No amount of visits in the intervening years had been enough to see that living at 'home' would be not merely a challenge but devastatingly hard.

My mother's eldest sister had always punctuated her conversation with local road names, those who lived there, and their relation to her. Someone named Marie lived on Serpentine Avenue, in a house two down from the man who owned a shop in Ringsend, and whose son married Marie's daughter who was in the choir my aunt sang in.

Someone else named Seamus, whom she met on holiday at Lake Garda, had lived all his life next to her nephew on Tritonville Road, which was a coincidence; he'd known the Murrays and the Conroys, too, had been married in the same church, but had himself moved to a new-build in Killiney that was on the road they'd always taken to Whiterock. My aunt's patter created a personal map based on her parish and the relationships between the people of a particular place, gradually extending outward, connecting even the distanced world to the minutely local.

But in a city as large and everchanging as New York, my mother had not relied on individuals and her connection to them to navigate. She used major structures: libraries, museums, churches, theatres. In her new Dublin seaside neighbourhood there were no such significant buildings. The roads curved unpredictably, unlike in the core of Manhattan where the grid and number system made location clear. You met your friend for lunch on the specifically southeast corner of 18th St and Irving Place. Or you met at the ground-floor information desk of the Guggenheim, or at the opera beneath the atomic chandeliers. Everything in her new space was low to the ground, and there was much more sky. At the seafront itself, that broad sky met the largeness of the sea. It must have seemed to her as if everything had been cleared away, as in the devastation of war.

Sometimes it seemed as though she was navigating with the accurate map of a place in which she was not present; I sensed as we paced and practised that, if we were in New York, her feet might have tracked to her usual walks along the river, to her usual stores. She might have ended up in her correct seats at the opera, turned up for Sunday brunch at the right time in the right place. She had the internal map of a city, but no longer lived there. And as an immigrant to Ireland myself I understood her hesitancy, still second-guessing my way. It was never as simple as gradually learning to situate the self in widening concentric circles, because both the place and the self continued to change.

In truth, even when she had been in New York the last year, her internal map had begun to break apart so that it was not always the case that she found herself in the correct seats, in the usual restaurant. When both the place and the self changed beyond memory and recognition, what resulted was catastrophic: the world turned to a maze without centre, without prospect of solution.

*

When the call came – how did people receive these pieces of news before phones? – I was in the garden with O. We had just returned from a long drive and he was fed up with the confinement of the car seat, the glare in his eyes; he needed time outside, with my full attention. Together we were wandering the garden, his chubby fingers testing strawberries, delightedly plucking sugar snap peas. The grass was growing shaggy and I contemplated cutting it after lunch, admiring the beautifully clear light of an Irish summer's day.

My mother had collapsed at lunch with other residents; perhaps she'd had a stroke, or a heart attack. The grass waved and glinted and I thought that I would upset my son by having to put him back in the car now. My mother's state was so uncertain that I did not know what to feel. There was, as there almost always is in such moments, a resulting stillness. In the glorious summer garden, skimmia and daphne scenting the air, I held in one hand the phone, and with the other was tugged from my motionlessness by a gorgeous, boisterous boy.

*

At my mother's bedside over the weeks of that summer, I wondered what to do: if and when she recovered, how would I manage to mind her at home and go to work, care for the children? But the doctors would not release her to me, a refusal which prompted me to feel at once bereft and grateful.

Various medical experts visited her daily, but I missed them, arriving too early or too late. Eventually one of the doctors called me. I took the call up a tree, at a zipline and climbing park where I'd taken my youngest and two friends before I'd have to return to my mother's bedside. The entire summer I felt I was snatching only occasional hours with the kids, calling upon friends to take them for playdates and activities while I sat with my mother and tried to figure out what to do.

I'd been trying to get this doctor on the phone for weeks, so I stood there on a platform high up in the summer oaks of Kilruddery, clipping myself in with one hand

and following the kids while the doctor gave me his prognosis. The sky was heavy, the branches thin and light and fringed with swaying green. The sound of the wind diminished and hushed up there amid the smaller leaves. You have your hands full, he told me, as if he could see me. He had noticed me carrying my youngest stealthily in and out of the room where no children were allowed, my older boy trying to hide behind my legs; he'd seen me other days when I whirled in from work and settled by my mother's bed with a laptop while she slept. She was curled into tight, awkward shapes that I'd never seen her in before.

I think of this doctor on occasion, his intervention in my life, in others' lives.

There were members of my family who had made decisions to move relatives into nursing homes. I had not judged them. Yet I felt judged and defensive; I criticized myself. What did it say about me that I couldn't see how I could continue to be myself, to work, be a parent – generally live – if I brought my mother home? Was it a failure of imagination? Of sympathy? Was it selfishness that led me to accept the doctor's words? I carried with me – perhaps still carry – the sense that my extended family believed I had failed my mother. By contrast, I knew that she, who had prized her independence like a hard-won medal, would not have chosen to live with me in that way.

When it was clear after weeks in hospital that my mother would not be returning to her apartment, I went there alone. At her door, the lavender we'd planted a year before was in flower, as were some pink dianthus and purple phlox Donal had chosen for their perfume. I deconstructed furniture to give away, re-boxed the remaining stuff.

Later, about a year after her death, as though coming round from a bout of amnesia, I found myself thinking of particular things that were my mother's and wondering where they were. Things that I now longed for and which could never be recovered. I had never expected, back in New York when we packed up the apartment, that I would continually think of a set of mugs given to my mother by an Irish potter, of how much they were attached to my images of my childhood: my mother at the table each morning, holding a mug of tea and doing the *New York Times* crossword. Where had the throw from the couch gone? Or the blanket at the end of my mother's bed, so unwieldy on the needles that she swore off cables and Aran knitting?

Other things that I pine for still: her marble rolling pin; a lidded basket in which she stored buttons, made for her by Jude, the Hopi man who befriended her when she arrived half heart-broken in Arizona; *The Joy of Cooking*, *Betty Crocker's New Picture Cook Book*, her first American cookbooks, annotated with translations of the measurements as she learned them; a wooden box with mother-of-pearl inlay in which she had once stored precious letters from home; my father's beige fabric-covered *Webster's Dictionary*, thick spine cracked from daily openings, weave visibly loosening, index notches softened by my parents' fingers.

I only came to feel these items' absence when my mother herself was gone. It's their everyday-ness that I miss, reminders in particular – because I had her in my life for so much longer – of my mother's presence. These were the very things that she left behind when she went out to work, or to rehearsals, or on a trip: a cup washed and left to drain by the sink, her bed neatly made and the blanket laid across the foot of her four-poster.

Where are these things and what did we do with them? I don't know and I don't remember, and to say so gives me the pain of loss. I can see myself leaving them out of the shipping boxes, reasoning that she would use them until she left and then, perhaps, carry them with her in suitcases on the final flight home. She did not.

The last time I was in her apartment in New York – several months before her return to Ireland – it was still fully functional and lived in, despite the fact that we were boxing up many items. Perhaps this is why I can occasionally conjure it, not as a stage deconstructed after a show but in some wholeness, as if the rolling pin and mugs are still in the kitchen, the cookbooks on a shelf – as if I could fly to New York and ask the doorman to let me in to retrieve what remained behind.

Most of the time, though, I am left to imagine the progress of those lost items, falling into hands in thrift stores, becoming part of other people's lives – scattered pieces of an intimate memory map that could also have made their way into the trash, because their meaning would, for strangers, lie only in their use.

Outside my mother's Dublin apartment I said goodbye to her neighbours, also retirees who liked to garden and read. They had been sweet and welcoming, initially inviting her in for cups of tea and games of cards, then just for cups of tea as it became apparent she could no longer manage cards; in return she had helped them to weed their flower beds as her knees were not as arthritic as theirs. It was warm, summer fighting on into autumn, the flowers persisting in their sheltered spots. The retirees came out as I moved final bags and boxes into the car; they sent good wishes. I felt awkward and sorry, aware that through the years they watched this process on repeat. Someone took ill or died and they saw a life re-boxed and removed from sight with remarkable swiftness. They must have thought inevitably of their own lives being re-boxed and removed. I wished I had come at night so that they did not have to see, so that I did not have to feel, how swiftly the traces of lives could be pushed from sight.

*

When my mother was diagnosed with vascular dementia it was on the basis of the brain scan from New York, though the assessment took place in Ireland a year later. My mother and I went in to see the doctor whose job it was to analyse the extent of the cognitive damage. It seemed unlikely that he was ever able to give good news. In his semi-basement office of the hospital he sat at a plain metal desk, which suggested how little time he spent on this part of his job.

It was like a film set: an office telephone, a small plastic tray that held blank paper. On the walls were shelves, but they were sparsely populated. In this plain room, with its uncomfortable, hard chairs and chill, damp smell, he asked patients a series of questions. It began as a conversation – introductions, niceties – before sliding into a type of quiz. My mother gamely played – in answer to his query about the year she laughingly told him that she was retired and didn't need to worry about time – but it was a spectacle that no one would wish to witness.

I was struck by his lack of gentleness, by the way in which he pursued her until she had no answer: then he would point this out. It was a technique he had pat, but the humiliation of it hurt me. I felt angry – just as I would later with the psychiatrist who believed both my mother and I were lying – at the need to cruelly expose someone I loved so dearly.

And yet his manner worked, his words took effect. As we left the basement office we discussed what he had said. I've had a good life, she told me, in tears in the car. The game had disappeared; she had heard the diagnosis and it entered her mind blade-like. We had coffee and cake somewhere, prolonging a return to her apartment, trying to move past what his words meant, making plans for the coming weekend with the children. But it was only a few weeks later that she collapsed. It was as if her mind, in coming to terms with what was happening, had stumbled further down the stairs rather than taking them one at a time.

*

My mother begged me to contact the assisted suicide place. Was it France? She couldn't remember. She'd begun to speak cruelly, in a way she had never done before, asking could I not call them for the love of God, do something useful for once in my life; these were favourite phrases. When myself and the children arrived to see her at the nursing home one sunny morning she screamed at us to get the fuck out.

My mother was a woman for whom *damn* was an expression of strong anger; famously among our extended family, the school of my mother and her sisters had had a code of behaviour that outlined 'the seven acts of rudeness'. One of these had been the use of 'bad language', and neither my mother nor her sisters could ever have been said to have broken the code – until now. I was still at the stage of trying to reason with her. I gestured to the children, whom she loved dearly and who loved her as much, saying that they'd wanted to see her, hoping to divert her attention back to the present and their expectant little faces. *Get the fuck out!* she repeated. I stood the children outside the room, explained to her quietly that I couldn't bring them in if she was going to speak like that. Her reply was to echo her new phrase again.

It was triumphant, this imperious discovery. In this new place of no maps, my mother could speak differently, could reinvent her relationship to us as if we also were unlocatable and so objects of no consequence. Had she, I wondered, withheld such words, such sentiment in her life, to let it explode out of her now? Or was this new language standing in for other words she had lost, other things like her sense of the external world? Was it in fact not standing for anything at all but her anger at being stricken with dementia?

She pounded her fists into the wardrobe, the wall, until her hands, with their translucent skin, were bruised with blood. She tore photos into iotas of data that would never again make sense as images. Her glasses, with their special lenses thickened and polished as her vision failed, were rent and smashed. In an instant, she could sweep a counter full of brochures and pens to the floor, consign her dinner to the lino with a gesture of her arm. The flashes emerged out of nothingness, out of a body smiling only a moment before. The doctors told me that it was a progression of disease, that a web was settling itself over once perfect cells of thought. But it was not only that. I was the decipherer of code, the translator of silence: I knew what the moments were and what they said. She was finally speaking, each pound of the fist a claiming of the past's anger, a rejection of inaction. After a lifetime of letting go, moving forwards – the American psychological clichés – she pushed back and enacted rage that she had once swallowed.

I left in tears, a child holding each of my hands. My oldest, then eight, was near tears himself, distressed by his grandmother's illness and rage, as well as for me. My youngest was cross. Still only four, his loyalties were roused and his small hand was tight on mine. Well, he said stoutly as we got outside, that didn't go very well!

I made the daily visits alone. I couldn't bear the thought that this version of her would dominate the children's memory, or that she would have the pain of occasional understanding that they were seeing her in this desperate state.

Almost every day my mother brought up what she called 'the place where you could die'. Sometimes she tearfully pleaded with me to take her there; other days she screamed with a fury that, like her cursing, was so out of character I felt helpless before it. After several bewildering weeks I contacted Dignitas by email, my enquiry at once bland (I was looking for administrative information) and desperate (my mother was asking me to help her end her life). But it was too late, as I'd suspected: with a diagnosis of dementia, she could make the decision no longer. The email was efficient and kindly; they'd heard it all before. After my mother's death a lawsuit made it possible for people to legally note their preference to die before a diagnosis had taken place or in the earliest stages, but this was years away, and her dementia too advanced, in any case.

One visit, after we'd walked for an hour and I'd managed to convince her to sit for a cup of tea, her mood spiralled, as it often did when she stopped moving. I don't want to be here, she announced, and I don't mean just *here* – she gestured around her pleasant room. I've had enough, as I keep telling you. For once in your life – she used her theatrical training to brilliant effect, pausing before the repetition – for *once in your life* can you not do what I wish? Instead of using her normal speaking voice, she projected during such speeches as if she were on the stage, so often heads turned or, as now, a carer might pop into her room to make sure all was well. I was useless for not doing as she wished, she ended, her voice trembling with anger. Exhausted, I told her quietly about what I'd found out. Generally I'd learned to abandon explanations as most failed to connect with her, but this one did: as if she was so earnest in her desire for death that a serious answer to this key question she absorbed immediately.

Thank you for trying, love, she said, in her ordinary voice.

She never mentioned it again. Soon, she had forgotten it as a possibility, though she may well have continued to wish to die.

*

Probably after consulting experts in the psychology of elder care, various stations had been set up as points of interest in the nursing home, laid out to trigger memories of childhood, say, or working life.

A wooden dollhouse with scanty furniture and no dolls sat on a shelf beneath a tableau of straw hats decorated with fake flowers. It was a stark contrast to my dollhouse and to the one that my children now had, furnished with the things I'd collected and inhabited by the same family of dolls: this one, despite its pretty paint job, spoke of abandonment, tragedy, emigration. An old typewriter was next to the dollhouse, without a ribbon, its metal legs of letters settled in place.

Another station had a sewing machine, a wooden jack-in-the-box, several large porcelain dolls, a photograph of Frank Sinatra that I suspected had come in the frame. One wall was covered with black-and-white images of movie stars meant to be from the era, I think, of the residents' youth, though these were from too far in the past to be appropriate. It was as if the past had been imagined as a static period that all generations accessed, one involving Greta Garbo, Fred Astaire. Another corner of the nursing home had a small but realistic-looking bar, replete with taps and a few metal-lettered signs typical of an Irish pub. Everywhere the floor was pale linoleum easily mopped, and the walls were lemon, peach, except near the bar, where they were darker beige, as if stained by years of smoke.

One of the worst phases during my mother's time in this nursing home was her compulsion to walk. The hallways were wide, imagined as internal boulevards for perambulations, not for the kind of maniacal walking that my mother was possessed to do (her compulsion would haunt me as I myself ran laps in various places). Never, in all of our miles of walking, did I see any resident pause to examine or interact with the carefully staged displays. Instead, only my youngest son stood and gazed intently into the dollhouse, mournfully noting the lack of inhabitants. He could not resist the keys of the typewriter or the listing clown of the jack-in-the-box. Otherwise, the displays gathered dust until, at a new season, they would be reinvented. My small son would quickly work out the new placements: the dollhouse and large dolls together, now, the typewriter alongside Frank Sinatra. Rather than drawing the residents' attention, these mise-en-scènes actually replicated and performed the emptiness of objects for most of them. The tableaux could have been comprised of any one of their possessions, a random box of things no longer of interest, no longer used, no longer recognized as one's own.

The depopulated dollhouse was an unintended representation of the homes the residents had themselves left behind, either let or sold up to pay for the expense of their care or returned to the rental market. The corridors along which the scenes were situated were nowhere, in-between spaces that contained objects without meaning; residents like my mother no longer assigned value to things at all, so the disembodied displays were eminently appropriate. My youngest child's persistent interaction with the tableaux caught sight of something uncanny in the way they'd been emptied of significance, and by playing with and touching them he seemed to be trying to offer them meaning. He felt sad for the dollhouse and worried where the people had gone, felt sorry for the toys unplayed with, the hats unworn. Unlike in a museum, these grouped objects had no history, no story to tell, and so my small son stood before them, repeatedly encountering something that troubled and fascinated him.

My mother swept by all of it. In New York it had been her habit to walk to and from work except in the dog days of steamy August; after she retired she went along the East River each morning for several miles, pausing for chats with other regulars. In horrid winter weather that kept her indoors, she met her old friend Joann at the health club to swim and talk in the sauna.

When she moved back to Ireland she was still fit and physically strong, which fed her compulsion to move. The difficulty was that she no longer recognized when to stop, when she had enough. Instead of walking for an hour in the morning as part of a social routine, she now set off as soon as she was awake and continued until something or someone stopped her. But perhaps this was her way of mapping space; her old habit of keeping fit now became the persistent need to figure out where she was, to find somewhere familiar.

In the time before the nursing home, she could and had become entangled in wrong turns and the fact that there was no clearly demarcated end; she could wander endlessly through a maze-like world and never finish her explorations. Inside, in the nursing home, she faced dead ends or locked doors, limited choices to turn one way or the other. Initially she knew her room, recognizing it by the photos on the walls and bedside table. But as her sight deteriorated she relied on some muscle memory, the endless repetition of finding herself there in the room again.

Within half a year, though, that homing in had vanished; she wandered through the nursing home with no recognition of a particular area or person, greeting people repeatedly with almost comedic politeness. If she was going nowhere, she was getting through time in a way that she could not get through space, propelling herself into the future step by step by step.

If I put on music that caught her attention – a choral piece that she had performed – and massaged her shoulders, sometimes I could coax her to sit. Other times she might be persuaded to pause for a few bites of lunch or, more often, sips of tea, occasionally a sweet. But even when she sat she bounced one leg over the other uncontrollably, until the tremors forced her to stand and move. We would set off again, once more saying hello to all of those we'd been passing in endless laps. She could no longer be termed an enthusiastic walker; she was now walking herself into nothingness, walking herself to death, as I saw it. Sometimes I wondered if, when the place she could die vanished as a possibility, something in her fixed on this new way of reaching the unreachable place.

But after a year and a half in the nursing home a new phase saw her forgetting to open her eyes and unable to follow a request to do so: in her mind, they were open already. To general consternation, she persisted walking blindly. After near-misses with residents who careened out of her way, and after several falls, she ended up in bed, continuing to bounce her leg ceaselessly, so that the carers and I regularly had to shift her back up towards the pillows. It was unsafe for her to walk, the doctor told me bluntly, unless she opened her eyes; she was a danger to residents, a danger to busy nursing staff, and of course a danger to herself.

And so the bed became a new space to which she was forced to adjust. I sat beside her in a chair. Her eyes were closed but moving beneath their thin lids, and she spoke as if they were open. I wondered where she was, what she was seeing as her body moved against the confinement: was she back in New York in a familiar place, or backwards in time in an Ireland that had not vanished? Or was she closing her eyes against all that was happening here?

Several times she moved so vigorously that her legs ended up lodged over the new safety rails and she cried out in pain, still bouncing her legs, but now against a wall.

There were weeks of this constraint, days and nights in which her limbs continued to attempt to walk.

As if the need for constant motion was not bad enough, she had been increasingly afflicted with intense hallucinations and paranoia that went beyond the more usual sundowning, which saw tired-out dementia patients' moods swoop towards day's end in sudden, erratic ways not unlike the crash-outs of exhausted toddlers. A psychiatrist specializing in dementia care came to see her in the days before she closed her eyes.

First, he walked with her, trying to gauge her mind's mechanisms; then he talked with me in an office borrowed from the nursing home's doctor to go through his notes. While we sat I was conscious of where my mother might be in the building, moving swiftly through the corridors: was she searching for me? He deemed her delusions so severe that he did not believe me when I said, answering his question, that she had never suffered from any psychotic illness before this. He looked at me pityingly, clearly believing that I needed the illusion of an earlier period of wellness.

She's just told me that she sang in Carnegie Hall, went on tour in China, and also that she used to work for an Irish government agency in New York, he said. That these things were all true seemed beyond him. Surely one of the saddest things about dementia, I felt then, looking at this sharp man in a suit, was that a person's ability to narrate their own life, to offer elements of themselves in conversation and to meet others' narrations with interest and curiosity, was removed from them. And if this doctor didn't believe me, who functioned as her living aide-mémoire, speaking on her behalf, then what?

But this doctor and I did not see the world in the same way. Why, I wondered, did it seem necessary to point out to my mother her delusions at all? Surely if she announced with delight that she'd just returned from Paris the only proper thing to do was to ask how the trip had been? After battling through my early impulse to explain and try to use logic, I now took the same tack I took with my children – engaging with flights of fancy and imaginative invention, but speaking seriously to reassure against concerns and fears.

Unfortunately, the trips to Paris were rare enough; mostly my mother was plagued with worries that people were spying on her, taking her things (which she'd given away), that terrible events were happening everywhere (not far off the mark). Her misery terrified me. My attempts at reassurance failed. I could do nothing about her agony. So when the doctor suggested antipsychotics to try to help stabilize her mood I agreed.

*

I had always admired my parents' quickness to enter into sympathy with other people's emotions and thoughts, something furthered by their practice as actors. Likely because of the loss of his mother and younger sister within a year of each other while he was very young, my father often felt things rather too deeply, the trauma and emotion he was not encouraged to express in the early 1940s surfacing. He had profound responses to music and sometimes wept while I practised the piano as a child, though I was in no way accomplished enough to evoke that level of emotion. Once, at a dinner party in our apartment when I was six or seven, he had gotten very drunk and, amid the usual sing-song and recitations, he broke down while someone sang a ballad about Michael Collins. I was in a favourite corner in our hallway beside a bookcase, reading on a pile of cushions, something I liked to do when my parents' actor friends came over. There in my nook, I could hear and engage with them if I wanted to, or just stay engrossed in my book until I was sent to bed.

Over and over again, my father said *Poor Michael Collins* and cried, to my mother's surprise and slight mortification; apparently he'd never before displayed such feeling for Collins or any other Irish nationalist figure. His tearfulness lasted long enough that I rose from my cushions to check on him. Another drunk actor sat with his arm about my dad's shoulders, the two of them having a low confab while the rest of the party moved on, guitars passing through hands, different fingers running over piano keys.

This incident became a standing joke amid their circle – my father himself later finding it hilarious that he'd been so overcome – but I always remembered it with a degree of concern, for like him I seemed to take on the hue of other people's emotions too readily: if not distraught by the assassination of a historical figure of national importance, moved to tears by others' sadness, overcome in relaying a story of someone's intense joy. It could be worrying to feel so much on behalf of others that one's own sense of self was telescoped, diminished.

While my mother suffered what seemed like unendingly, I felt a wildness in my body; the result of an attunement to her moods, her physical and mental state. It felt sometimes like a reverberating echo of what she was going through passed through me, as if we were on opposite sides of a canyon and she had let go of an unbridled scream that, cartoon-like, hurtled towards me, the figure watching closely from the opposite edge.

*

In this way my mother and I endured hours and days and weeks and months and years.

*

In her illness I had come to carry memory for my mother; I functioned at times as her map, her voice, her narration of self. But I also held her actual memories, particularly as she herself was freed of them, as if they emptied from her mind into mine. A far more profound inheritance than the objects she had given away.

Having grown up with a parent who narrated the past so beautifully and who nurtured the memory of those she loved, I felt the significance of this transfer. I had listened, rapt, as my mother described what seemed to an urban only-child like me a wondrous childhood by the sea, surrounded by siblings and extended family. I was her perfect audience, full of the peculiar child-of-immigrant longing to belong where I lived but also to the place of my parents, aware that I fully belonged to neither.

Her stories conjured Ireland for me while we sat in our Manhattan high-rise overlooking the East River and the lines and strata of midtown. When she bought me dresses in Macy's, she spoke of the dresses she and her sisters had designed and sewn for tennis- and rugby-club dances; she showed me black-and-white photos in which she and her sisters wore pale gloves to their elbows, and then revealed from a drawer a pair of the gloves themselves into which I slid my child's hands. I marvelled at the cool white fabric and the fact that they fit in no way into my own life. She described the making of jams from jewels of summer fruit in their long back garden, the plucking of rhubarb stalks with a snap from their crowns, and I considered the mounds of fruit differently when next we walked to the farmers' market, suddenly aware that, unlike my mother, I could not imagine the fruit's actual growth, only conjure its pyramidical presence on stalls around the city.

It seems strange to say that in the metropolis of New York my mother made the world bigger with her stories of suburban seaside Dublin, but this is what happened. She passed to me story after story, most seemingly inconsequential in that they were about the day-to-day of their family life, about the preparation of food, the celebration of birthdays and holidays. In sharing these pieces of her experience, which were also expressions of loss, she gave me the profound sense of life being comprised of those details, of the seemingly inconsequential.

I was enchanted by my mother's endless flow of stories, which extended beyond her own family life into a deep appreciation for the song, literature and mythology of Irish culture. Tales like 'Deirdre of the Sorrows', the pronunciation of Irish words and phrases, books of small square black-and-white photos that were tiny channels into the past, the recitation of poetry from medieval to modern; all counted as part of that flow, part of her memory.

I drifted to sleep while she sang, not just childhood rhymes and lyrics, but also '*Báidín Fheilimí*' and 'I Dreamt I Dwelt in Marble Halls', on occasion 'Danny Boy', the song she was most requested to perform at get-togethers and the afters of weddings. Songs gathered to her after emigrating – Gershwin's 'Summertime', Joni Mitchell's 'Both Sides Now' – also rotated in. Something in the longing notes haunted me, presented me with fragments of feeling that weren't mine, weren't necessarily hers either, but were part of some larger state of longing: homesickness, lovesickness.

In retrospect, and as a parent, I know that it was only with me, her child, that she could have shared this weight of memory. It was deeply private and personal, speaking slant of her sometimes terrible loss, the sometimes inadequacy of what had replaced that life; it would have been unthinkable to say this to someone who would have responded with anything but a child's ready acceptance.

My mother had made a happy life for herself in the United States, determinedly, because, as she often said to me, she was a happy person. But I knew that at times, at certain moments, the longing for home, for the lost life she thought she would lead, gripped her remorselessly. The pain in the knowledge that time and space away from beloved people could never be recovered she expressed through her singing and through her stories. As with other parents who say such serious things to small children sometimes, she would not have been aware of how deeply embedded it became in my mind, or how the word *home* for me was not associated at all with my own life, with our own home, but with hers, the absence of it.

She had always talked of going home. For vacation, yes, those all-too-brief weeks when we left the overheated city behind and arrived in the surprisingly cool and bright breezes of Irish summer. At the airport she and her sisters erupted into joyous laughter at the sight of one another, and at the end of the month their faces ran with tears. Even as a small child I often cried as well, overcome with the sadness of those farewells. Yet I knew too that though she wept she would stop; she would mop at her eyes with tissues after security, on the plane. After the then-required stopover at Shannon, she would, despite the clinging of that raw sorrow, put me before herself, play small games of cards on the tray tables of the plane, begin to talk of what we would do and who we would see when we reached the other home of New York.

My dad would be waiting for us, she said. It would still be warm and we would go to Jones Beach with friends. It would be exciting to get ready for a new year at school: to buy pencils and sharpeners and to cover the books with pretty contact paper. She would whisper-sing me to sleep as we crossed the Atlantic. *We'll be okay, love, we always are*, she'd say.

*

Early on in her illness she had lashed out in anger about my father. Her tone was more distressing to me than hearing the facts of how my father's drinking had led to the loss of their first house: a straight narrative of what had happened didn't have the raw, wounded quality of her voice, couldn't reflect how stricken she must have been in putting first one and then the other foot into the body of a plane that would transport her away from her life, away from her family.

The anger, like the cursing, astonished me. Once an outburst reduced me to sudden tears. He was my father, I said to her, explaining my reaction. Damn him, was her reply. But she slipped from this angry phase and surprised me one day by telling me when I arrived that my dad was already home and had baked bread. He's always very kind, my mother said, her face placid.

Now, as she lay dying, she no longer exhibited any remembrance of anger, of coming to terms, or of her love for my father. I'd sat beside her and accepted her flow of memories, and they seemed to have almost run out.

EATING AND DYING

When I asked Nancy what she wanted me to bring in to the hospital she said fruit cocktail. The tinned kind, with florid cherries that pinken pears and bloodstain peaches. It was 3 January and it turned out there was none available. I tried Centra, SuperValu and Dunnes, texting updates because we always texted updates.

Nothing in Roundwood, I thumbed, *but it's tiny*. Then, *Out in SuperValu too. Have mandarin segments.*

Wtf? she replied. *Why is there a run on fruit cocktail?*

A floor manager in Dunnes figured it. Must've been a lot of trifle had for New Year, he said. Sure you have that to keep you going – he gestured to the plastic tray of chilled watermelon slices in my hands – and I'll have another lot in on the Monday.

It was Friday. Nancy would be dead before the new shipment of fruit cocktail was unloaded out the back of

Cornelscourt in the cold, by lads not altogether sorry to be back at work after headbanger holidays.

*

When, decades ago, my father was dying in a New York hospital, I arrived at the desk and they could not locate him; he was in transit, being moved to give us privacy that final day. And as a teenager not yet burdened with consciousness of how death could impact the psyche, I did something eminently practical: went to the hospital café and ordered lunch, returning to the desk fifteen minutes later to be told his room number. I sat in the canteen, taking a number of bites before becoming ashamed that I was eating a burger while my father was dying. I pushed it aside, drinking the coffee instead. I still feel the tingle of embarrassment about it. When my mother was dying two decades later, I knew not to do this to myself. For days before her death, I drank the tea that nurses and carers insisted on bringing me, but didn't eat the biscuits, small packets of gingernuts, custard creams and digestives. I put them into my backpack so as not to seem ungrateful.

By the time Nancy died, I didn't even have tea. My throat was dry when I left the last day, my head light with hunger.

MOVING TOWARDS DEATH

The summer that marked Nancy's last before her illness, she travelled home to the US with her daughter for a month-long holiday. We met in Glendalough with the kids the week before her departure, walking to the lake with Aoife; kids, dogs and adults moving in a chaotic, ragtag group. There was ice cream and the feeding of ducks, drizzle and sun, children's knees grazed from racing too hard on the forest path, shoes and shorts sodden from unplanned paddling in the cold lake.

There was also Nancy's anxiety about the fact that, with only days to go until her flight, she had ended up with an unusual complaint. A pot had come out of the dishwasher with a small bit of pasta stuck to its bottom, and in trying to scrape it out, the hardened piece wedged under her nail. It had snapped in her attempts to grasp it in tweezers, prompting a visit to the doctor. He suggested that it would either grow out in the coming weeks, or, if it showed signs of infection, the nail would need to be removed. Her finger was sore and the nail contorted, but she was going to go ahead and fly home and hope for the best. New words to live by: never scrape at stuck spaghetti, she repeated to all of us, half laughing; what a stupid thing to happen.

When she returned to Ireland, we met once more in Glendalough in the days before school began, walking this time up to the mining village. We progressed through the strange landscape of the ruined houses, past the rusted hulks of machinery from a century ago that were like industrial art installations amid the granite of the valley floor. The sharp faces of the cliffs rose around us and we pointed out climbers on a multipitch way above, and also goats, moving easily up and down the steep inclines.

My youngest son had broken an arm while Nancy was away and he was in a cast, recovered enough to be annoyed by its constancy. Despite O's cast, the kids scrambled up boulders and examined pieces of quartz crystal, occasionally pocketing a preferred piece; my mother had many times palmed similar shards of white and clear crystal on this walk.

While the kids roamed, Nancy talked about the homesickness that inevitably hung over her in those initial few days back in Ireland. It was one of the reasons we'd met that day, so that I could console her, help her adjust back to her Irish life. She mentioned, in that undone village, in that spare space of granite and sliding stone, that her stomach hurt. The discomfort, like intense indigestion, she said, did not diminish while we walked, more slowly than usual, so after a time we turned back, rounding up the kids from their explorations. We left the stone valley behind for the sway of the tall pines at the lake's edge, the trail soft with needles. The air was warm and sticky; it felt like summer was ending, that the coming rain would take away the remaining warmth and plunge us into autumn.

At the carpark we parted. Nancy and her daughter and their dog drove off while I urged my boys into our car. I was uneasy enough that Nancy and I texted a dozen times that night. She felt more and more uncomfortable; she promised she would go to the doctor the next day. But in the morning she was in more pain and didn't want to drive. Her husband would be home from work that evening, she said, and they would go to the hospital if she still felt unwell. She joked that she was adjusting to not having American food again: her stomach mourning the lack of vegetarian Reuben sandwiches until the next trip home.

I didn't think to ask about the spaghetti in her nail until a year later. When I did, she said, God, remember when I was worried about a bit of pasta?

*

Nancy's formal diagnosis with stage 4 ovarian cancer came when my mother was fluctuating between deathbed and reprieve: though she had once more opened her eyes, my mother was bedbound, almost unspeaking, still. She hardly talked now except to croak out a *hello love* when I came in. Occasionally she would cry gently for her mother and I would immediately begin to croon *there there, love, mammy's here*, sometimes for an hour at a time.

One day I broke off, put my head down on the edge of her bed and sobbed, unable to speak. After a few moments her hand fumbled awkwardly near my hair, trying to console me. It was just what a small child might do on witnessing a parent in extremis, silently and gently touching to provide comfort; and yet, of course, it was also as if her parental instinct had been sparked by my weeping. I wondered if in her confusion she thought it might even have been me, moments before, calling aloud for my mother.

*

Early autumn days were bookended by stops at Nancy's on my way to work, and on my way home at my mother's bed in the nursing home near Brittas Bay. Weeks passed of sitting beside my mother and singing and talking to her. Gradually her bones emerged from her body in sharp contrast to her beautiful papery skin.

I stroked her hands, massaged them with balm, stroked her temples. She had always caressed my face with such gentleness: during childhood, at any time I'd been in crisis, in tender greeting or farewell. Friends whose families were not as affectionate often remarked on the fact that she called me *love*, which was common in Ireland but striking in an American context where 'honey' dominated and where many friends referred to their parents by name.

As I saw my mother's skeleton begin to assert itself, as I held her hands, I found phrases, memories, images of a eulogy forming in my mind. It did not feel morbid. It felt, instead, like a readying for what I knew was coming. I was aware that it would be difficult to do justice to her, to find a way to account for her life, and so it felt not only preparatory but important. I was comforted by how much there was to say about her, and by how dear she was to me.

Perhaps I struggled to put the phrases together initially because my earliest relation to her had been wordless, and my feelings for her had started beyond language, before it, during a time when my sense of her was in my ability to clutch and hold on, to be held. I thought often of Dorothea Brooke, that great *Middlemarch* heroine: 'the effect of her being on those around her was incalculably diffusive'. My mother had also 'lived faithfully a hidden life', giving up her career as a singer and actor for an office job when I was school age, wanting stability for me. She had turned down major roles that might have been career-defining, explaining to more than one director that her life had changed, that she found joy in creating a family home after long believing she could not have a child.

When she told me these stories in my teens I was aghast at the idea that she had given up opportunities because of me. I don't regret it at all, she always said. I had you. I can't say that I believed her, then; I wondered if she told me out of a sense of brimming longing, wanting me to know that things might have been otherwise. Only as I lost her, in the years that I was growing into parenthood, did I understand that pride could be taken in what one turned away from out of love.

*

The consolations of memory, though, were now beyond her. That she turned down a part opposite Al Pacino or a national tour with James Broderick, that she'd come to see singing in various choral groups as a much-loved hobby rather than a professional exercise: such things had long drifted away. And so, in her presence, holding her thin-boned hands with their freckles and knuckles and seizing grip, I thought about her eulogy.

Eulogizing is an organizing of facts: a way of deconstructing death, or of reconstructing a life. As many parents do, my mother had presented her past life in stories for me. There was a narrative of how she came to the United States, of her Irish theatre days; there were tales of American life, American theatre. People within her story had their own dramas, too; my mother was never concerned only with herself.

But what I realized was that she had told all of these things differently as I got older, had given me more information, casting light onto some fact, some tiny element that had seemed inconsequential before but now stood star-like at the centre of her construction. The past could be organized and reorganized in different patterns, a night sky of objects seen at different times, in different conditions.

*

One signal of my mother's impending death was the transformation of her room by two carers. I returned one morning to find that they'd strung up pink lights with tiny bulbs wreathed by stiff silk flower petals. A bedside lamp had been replaced with a candle. Next to it, knowing my mother's faith, they'd stood a small wooden cross of a kind that had once likely been in every home in Ireland. Afterwards I would think of this cross and wonder where it was stored between deaths. There was also an old-fashioned, cut-glass vase on the windowsill with scented pink carnations and baby's breath, which touched me: they knew that I'd refreshed her flowers each week, but I hadn't thought of it in the tumult of those days. Dimly lit by the warm glow of the fairy lights, lent a solemnity by candle and cross, the air of the room changed.

When she'd moved into the nursing home, the only things I decorated her room with were photographs, since these seemed to be the only things to hold her interest. I brought in these pictures, our nettipattam, trying vaguely to code a nondescript space into something personal and specific. After the photographs, other than fresh flowers and the ability to play the music that she loved, I paid little attention to her room. It was pleasant enough, with a view of a courtyard and planters that she helped to fill with pansies and geraniums. Despite my lack of interest in the surroundings, I remember with profound gratitude those gestures of redecoration as my mother began moving towards death; I remember the same two carers who cried through the funeral; I remember my wonderment, standing in the changed room, the vague warmth of the fairy lights.

It's a curious thing to do, to pay attention to the external elements of the world when it would seem pointless. Decorating is an investment, a sign of futurity, and I could no longer see a future for my mother, stuck in a present that was painful, consuming. But just because I couldn't see her future didn't mean that there wasn't one: she continued to live, to go on, inching her way forward in time despite profound discomfort and the collapse of her capacity for enjoyment.

That the carers decorated surprised me. At moments when nothing else matters but the people before us, when we ourselves cannot spare attention to our own comfort, that someone thinks to create a particular atmosphere for us in our pending grief is strangely humbling. It's not certain that my mother would have noticed if she had to die beneath the white-hot light of an industrial tubed bulb, but perhaps she and I both might have felt less peaceful, me sitting there watching her wrestle with her body; perhaps I would have remembered that the harsh light discoloured her skin, amplified the distance opening up between us. As if they anticipated my retrospection, the carers altered things just enough to liberate the days of my mother's dying from all of the preceding days of pain and unhappiness in that room. So accustomed to death, they were not calloused by it; they saw my mother's state and took the opportunity of my absence to ensure that a different atmosphere would prevail.

In contrast to the one my father died in, my mother's dying room had no view. The curtains were drawn; other people could have been walking in the courtyard, even sitting there in autumn sunshine, and it would have been disconcerting, I imagine, to see into this scenario from without. In any case, had the curtains been opened there would have been no vista through that window, no cityscape or expanse of country, nothing to draw the eye. Unlike during the hours of my father's death, though, I could hardly bear to look away.

Whereas with my father I had studied the idea of death through large windows that did not open, contemplating his impending absence by puzzling my eyes over the strange patterns of the city, with my mother there was no need for contemplation, no need to puzzle it out: her absence would be immense. I knew that much. Instead of looking elsewhere, I looked to her, thinking only that in a short time I would no longer be able to see her in physical form.

*

The eulogy I gave at my mother's funeral was long by usual standards. I wrote it in two attempts, sitting on a favourite couch, most of it in a torrent the afternoon after she died. The stove was lit. My husband was home, the kids as well. I felt safe and warm and surprised that I was not disintegrating. I tried to touch on the most important things for her. Her loving family life growing up. Singing. Music. The theatre. Sandymount. My dad. Moving to America and beginning a new life, with more singing, more theatre. Having a baby after she had accepted her childlessness, as she accepted with grace so much else in her life. Her love of travel, her volunteerism.

That the eulogy was so long did not concern me: I was writing it for her and for myself. After all, it would be delivered in a church in a townland in which she'd never lived, at a Mass by a priest she'd never known. Her many friends were mostly in New York and the west coast of the US; few were still alive in Ireland. Most of her immediate family had already died: only one sister, beloved and closest in age, would be there, having to bear the loss of her final sibling. There would be a handful of cousins, many of whom had stayed with her, with us, in New York through the years, but most had no special relationship with her or insight into her fuller life. I expected to speak this eulogy to my husband and children, mostly – I was thinking of them, too, while I wrote. I knew that they would accept my love and my loss and the downpour of words.

When we pulled in to the small churchyard I saw, to my surprise, some of my own friends stepping out of cars. It moved me to silence. I'd been so engrossed in the process of my mother dying that it did not occur to me that anyone would come to the funeral for my sake. It would never have occurred to me to ask anyone; you don't invite people to funerals.

I remembered it afterwards, the feeling of wordlessness that their presence evoked. I was used to speaking off the cuff in classes, accustomed to the need to *have* to speak because it was part of my job, even though I often felt shy or uncertain or just quiet. But seeing friends there to support me produced a pressure in my throat, made me wonder for the first time if I would really be able to deliver the eulogy; their presence meant that she really was dead, my mother, that the words and phrases I'd thought about uttering needed now to be said. It opened up a new grief that made me want to swallow words, keep them to myself. But I also wanted to do this particular thing for my mother, to speak of her, to voice publicly the abiding love that had been between us.

And so I narrated elements of my mother's life in the small church to people who had not known her, spotting as I spoke the crying carers, the small faces of my beautiful children nestled into their dad's sides, family members who had travelled to be there, and, somewhere right in the back, a fleeting glimpse of Nancy's husband.

*

If I'd felt guilty for experiencing a sense of profound loss while my mother was alive, I'd also felt it was necessary that I begin to work at my grief. I had to apply myself to it, try to face it little by little, edge my way into a room before turning to face whatever I would see in the mirror. I was privately, ashamedly afraid that without her I would fall apart, that I was wholly unprepared – that my sense of self was so mixed up in my closeness to her that, once she was gone, I would collapse.

Sometimes I would catch myself driving to the office, having brought the kids to school and dropped into Nancy afterwards, already calculating how late it would be when I'd be driving home to see my mother, and I would wonder how I was able to do these things, to perform like a functioning adult; it didn't occur to me that I was one for a long time. In fact, in some ways that realization came only when my mother had died, in the moment when I called Donal to tell him and said in answer to his question that yes, I was okay to drive home alone, the surprised feeling that this was true.

EPISODES OF LOSS

In the immediate swirl of grief there is the shock, the sense that no death or loss can be compared to another. But as with other rare experiences, the mind attempts to process them, looking for similarities, mining out distinctions. We begin to compile episodes of loss, farewell, funerals. I think of what it was like that first time, watching my father die. And I think of how, when my mother was dying twenty years later, it was as if the moments were suddenly parallel, channels of loss dug in on either side of me.

GLEAMS OF GLASS

Nancy refused hospital visitors over her two years of illness. Initially, while a diagnosis was pending, her husband and child went in together, spending long, drawn-out days first in a public ward with several other patients, and later in a private room in which the days were still long and drawn out. But as tests were performed and the stay in hospital stretched from days to weeks, only her beloved husband was allowed to see her. Concerned about the ongoing impact of the medical environment on her child, she was also mortified by the new exposure of her body in the public sphere and could not countenance anyone unnecessarily seeing her.

Her mortification was enhanced by an American tendency towards prudishness as well as by the ongoing struggle with her body, which now swelled with ascites – *cancer juice*, she came to call it. My mother's physical self had been consistently diminishing, moving towards a vanishing point as she strode and strode with singular focus. It gave her a manic, improbable, wiry strength. By contrast, in her illness Nancy's body loomed larger, the processes at work within her cells demanding more and more space, creating cascade effects that saw her organs surrounded by that *cancer juice*.

The engorgement moved and spread unpredictably: her stomach distended itself in a way that fed into a bodily shame complex so intense that to see Nancy was to be overcome with pity, her agony about how she felt and looked written in her expression. The distension could extend to a hand, to the legs, one side of the neck. It began to seem like a cartoon version of hammering down one pest only for another to pop up, and another, and another, an invisible multiplication process under the skin making it impossible to predict where next an issue would arise. She texted the details each day. And Nancy's engorgement was not something that she could run from, for she quickly became so ill as to be almost entirely immobilized. What for her was the indignity of these strange swellings was worsened by being unable to move. After a well-meaning friend arrived at the hospital without invitation in those early days, Nancy cried on the phone afterwards about how even her ability to close a door had been taken away. She requested that I text the new group chat: there were to be no visitors bar her husband.

Instead, we spoke on the phone daily, often several times a day; often she cried, pinned to a bed by the very weight of her illness. And, of course, unlike my mother, Nancy could articulate her state of mind, admitting to anger at her body as it had turned on her so newly, taking over in a way that wasn't so much foreign as overwhelming. Nancy had often been at war with her physical self. She and I had both come of age in an America obsessed with aerobics, sugar-free and diet products; I hadn't realized until adulthood how buffered I was by having immigrant parents who liked to cook and who had little interest in TV. Certainly in the decade I had known Nancy, a consistent percentage of our conversations focused on how a diet was going, how much weight she aimed to lose, what foods she could eat, and what she would eat on 'treat days', which meant a great deal to her. She couldn't seem to see that she was beautiful already; she treated her body like something that required domination.

But something shifted with her illness. Rather than Nancy warring with her body, her body now warred with her. It was strange to see such different paradigms: my mother's body outperformed her mind while Nancy's mind outperformed her body, and in both cases there was an unsettling gap where I had never believed in one before. As a student I had struggled to grasp the philosophical insistence on a split between body and mind, since I was fortunate enough to be so settled in my own form as to naively believe it intrinsic to my thinking, to my experience of the world. I'd even come to somewhat despise Beckett's novels for that very reason. But now, middle-aged, I was faced with two nightmarish versions of the Cartesian dilemma. It seemed one of those torrid childhood games of choice, which would you rather, where any choice is a condemnation of happiness. Both my mother and Nancy had been divided by illness from their sense of self. In a rush of abashed understanding, I knew that to feel settled in myself, to feel body and mind conjoined, was, in many ways, to reside in full health.

I listened to Nancy in those first weeks, hearing and receiving by text, email, voice memo and photo daily progress on tests, plans, and prognoses. By way of return I read articles and scrolled through forums, making forays into the new linguistic world of cancer treatment. I sent lists of questions for doctors, or processed information so that I could discuss it with Nancy. This continued for several weeks until her body had been stabilized in ways that allowed her to go home. That stabilization included the administration of tests invasive and non, the prescription of many medications, an official diagnosis of cancer, the tallying of a treatment plan and, finally, a first round of chemo.

The homecoming, much envisioned and longed for, was, unsurprisingly, harrowingly difficult. If she had left the house for a visit to the emergency room not knowing what was wrong other than that she was experiencing increasing unease and a solidity in her stomach that could be compared only to Braxton Hicks' contractions, Nancy returned to her house with stage 4 ovarian cancer, the prospect of chemo for weeks on end, and then, once that was endured, the promise of surgery to attempt to extract as much of the cancer as possible. There was no welcoming party and no sense of having achieved an *after*; instead, there were new medical props and a new language to speak.

That first hospital stay had been humbling, she said over and over again. The exposure of her body so wholly, its treatment as an object for scrutiny and the unearthing of a narrative which she had not herself written – this changed her. For the first time in her life she had come up against something that she could not act upon herself; there was no fix, no plan of action she could take that would change the outcome. For a person who had her whole life exhibited initiative, incentive, motivation, a willingness to change up and act in response to new opportunities or events, someone acculturated to the American belief in the individual will and her ability to achieve, this was shocking. And she was too ill to try, in any case, submerged in a chasm of pain and nausea, fever and immobility that was equally shocking in its depth.

Homecomings are so often disruptive experiences: the pined for, much imagined space of the home blurs under the strain of longing. The moment of return results in a painful reckoning of what was imagined or remembered confronting what is. Nancy longed for her bed, an oasis free of IV lines and monitors, a room into which no nurse or doctor would come with a circle of trainees to gaze at her. She would be able to sleep uninterrupted, to eat what she wished instead of the trays of bland hospital food (and attempts to accommodate her fussy vegetarianism that disliked an array of individual vegetables). Her daughter would be there and they could talk and listen to music and watch their shows together once again. The house would wrap her in its familiarity, its particularities – the art, the photos, the American food displayed on the counter – and she would be comforted by being back in the presence of her family, her pets.

But the reality was that she was too weak to climb the stairs to the comfort of her own room, and had to resign herself to the rented bed in the sitting room. In hospital she had longed for the *before*, which had swiftly taken on not just a nostalgic hue but a sense of the magical. The ordinariness of that time – fretting about how best to mark her child's birthday, deciding what to have for dinner, even missing elements of her previous American life, especially her family and friends – loomed like a fever dream.

Entering the house meant considering that she could not return to the state she existed in; the crossing of the threshold contained the blunt realization that she was not the same, that the past was gone. Even more than that, she was accompanied by the dawning fear of being in a room without IVs and monitors, nurses and doctors. She had wished for this non-medicalized space, longed for it in the stretched time of the hospital. But now the thing she had desired produced deep unease. Like the stereotype of a new parent going home with a baby terrified at the idea that someone has just put them permanently in charge of an infant, Nancy was confronted with a very new worry.

Home had suddenly become somewhere marked by the absence of expert medical staff who could react to any emergency. Her body had become so unpredictable that it was like a separate entity, something she regarded with absorbed anxiety and a creeping terror. It wasn't *like* a horror film; it was the same narrative as one, in which an intruder makes their way into the sanctity of the home and makes it impossible for the residents to rest comfortably there ever again.

She couldn't quite describe all of these feelings, would just say that everything felt weird, different, not the same. The drugs necessary to keep her alive and work on the cancer distanced her from key parts of her identity. Her responses to various medicines were never pleasurable and didn't provide identifiable relief. Some of them worked to dull pain or to temporarily stall the nausea that was the plague of her existence. But they never paved a way back to the woman who'd prided herself on her daily walks with the dogs, beachcombing for sea glass, the making of art in her pretty blue-painted studio shed where there'd once been a patch of back garden. At a far distance was the voluntary work she was involved in, and, though surrounded by signs of her musical career – the piano in her eyeline from the bed, the guitars and ukulele in a far corner – it seemed as if the person who had sung and played for joy was in a mirror, and she was powerless to reach her.

It was within her power, though, to accept visitors at home: she could control who came and went. With her mother and sister when they could fly over for visits, I was among that handful of people admitted to her bedside during the bad times. In the earliest days of her illness I came to collect her daughter, to bring meals, help her choose wigs, plan what needed to happen next, often as mere distraction from *the same four walls*.

Later on, when she was uneasy left alone with oxygen tanks and hazy on when to take what medication, I came to babysit, as she put it, while her husband was at work. Then I would talk with her, cook something she might feel she could eat (apple crumble, but also scones or sugar cookies), but often I just sat quietly in the dining room at the table with my laptop, working while she dozed on the hospital bed, the fulcrum of their living room.

The bed, delivered in a rush when we realized that she was being allowed home, meant that Nancy lived almost permanently downstairs, in the more public spaces of the house. An avid collector of work by Irish craftspeople and artists, Nancy's walls were hung with felt landscapes, needlepoint, watercolours, as well as personal items like a handwritten playlist from a favourite gig she'd done. There were display cases that showed off her best beach finds: swirling Codd marbles, glass bottle stoppers, smooth-edged pieces of sea pottery whose origins she'd researched.

Nancy wasn't a fan of history or fiction. Out of loyal friendship she'd painstakingly read a novel I wrote, a few pages a night; I have no doubt she found it taxing. She preferred biographies of musicians, but her searches for information about fragments of glass or porcelain delivered to shore involved archival work and puzzle-making of a kind that reminded me of the construction of a story.

She'd unearthed the tale of a Greystones hotel whose closing seemed to have prompted a staff member to fling its remaining crockery to the base of a cliff; she regularly found elements of plates, saucers, the spout of a teapot. A fellow beachcomber had scooped a section of a Spode plate from the *Titanic*, the fragment having negotiated the North Atlantic for a return journey. Her own favourite finds included a bottle throat over a century old and a particular marble spotted by her eagle-eyed daughter. Nancy loved these small things that the sea presented to her, loved presenting them in turn to those who visited her home.

Nancy had become obsessed with sea glass and sea pottery. I don't know how it began – on which visit to the shore it started. She found first one piece, then another. Her child was small and loved being on the beach; it was a natural thing to do, to bend to collect the gleams of glass from among grey stones, white and coral-coloured shell. If at first she took with her every piece she picked up, she quickly became more discerning, preferring glass fully clouded by the aggressions of surf over time, tossing back those pieces that were not yet ready; she never ceased to relish the finding of a marble. The house was full of glass fragments: in completed artworks, works in progress, bowls of gradations of colour or shape.

In addition to the artwork were signs of another preoccupation food from her American past. The kitchen usually contained a visible pile of various products: Pop Tarts, Lucky Charms, Kool-Aid, marshmallow fluff and, seasonally, candy corn for Halloween, matzah for Passover, Hershey's Kisses in green and red foil for Christmas, tins of sour cherries for hamentaschen at Purim. Just as my mother had returned to New York at the close of each summer laden with Barry's Tea, sides of salmon and wholemeal flour for making brown bread, Nancy requested the familiar items of her earlier life from visiting friends and family.

This brightly packaged pile signalled an American past wholly different to my own, which had been as the daughter of immigrants who cooked everything from scratch and avoided the garishly marketed processed food that filled the supermarket shelves of my childhood. (The only things in nature that would turn your teeth black are dirt and charcoal, my mother told me when I once asked if we could try Oreos.) Other times she treated herself by ordering from an American food supplier in Ireland, relishing the filling of the virtual shopping cart from a selection of snacks, sweets and treats of various kinds. The visibility of the items in her kitchen – they were not put away, or stored behind doors – suggested Nancy's need to keep her Americanness in sight, to retain it on this new map she'd been drawing in Ireland over a decade and a half.

The house showcased her personality, history, and absorptions in ways that I found curious, since they were exaggerated: no one who knew her could walk in without realizing that it was her home. You knew Nancy was in the room. Her speaking voice was loud by Irish standards, if not by American, and she sang with power in an unexpected, richly melodic voice. She was not old enough, as my mom was, to have reached the era of letting go of possessions or of being comforted by them. But at that stage she didn't know that she was on her deathbed, the only piece of furniture or decoration in the house that she hadn't chosen herself.

*

I had been at deathbeds, and found I did not fall apart. I could repeat to my father over and over again that we were there, that we loved him. I could sing to my mother, embark unselfconsciously on long monologues of memories that I knew were important to her. I could cry and talk, sing and talk, and I did not feel any embarrassment doing these things in the presence of doctors, orderlies, other visiting relatives. This was something that surprised me about myself.

*

Nancy sent her husband to my mother's funeral. Not long home from hospital, her immune system battered by chemo, she didn't dare leave the house. Instead, I visited her a few days afterwards. She presented me with a needlepoint hoop she'd embroidered (for in her illness she still had to create), four flowers with a bee hovering over them. Your family, she said, and your mom. We both cried. My grief for my mother mingled with a fearful grief for Nancy that bubbled lava-like in my stomach. I remember thinking that she must be acutely aware of the nearness of death, but we didn't discuss it. She told me how lovely her husband found my eulogy. He'd tried to record it for her but the result was garbled by church echo. She asked me to send it on; I gave her the pages with reluctance. How could she read them and not think of the words that might follow in her wake?

*

When my father became ill, I was young and there was no internet. People did not Google symptoms, diagnoses, prognoses as they do so swiftly now. There were no online medical resources, only old-fashioned encyclopaedias, libraries with their narrow wooden drawers of card catalogues. The only information we had was delivered to us by doctors. The workings of the body were truly mysterious to me, illness as serious as cancer incomprehensible. Doctors told my mother and father what would happen and we waited for it to happen, then waited for more news.

By the time my mother became ill, I relied often on the internet to interpret phrases and words, to give me predictions, to accept the search terms I poured into it. With a printout of her brain scan and its medical language, I sifted through the results until I knew, before the doctor's professional interpretation, that she had dementia. And after that, through those years, I searched names of medicines she was prescribed, looking at counterindications, trying to keep track of how one drug might interact with another and what that might mean for her symptoms.

By the time Nancy was ill, I wished that I had studied medicine and even looked up what would be required of me to switch careers. I took to reading medical journals, looking at scans on websites designed for oncologists. I sought out new studies and trials. For an academic researcher, this was natural to a degree, even if the area I was reading about was so far from my own. And as her friend, it also felt natural that I would use what small capacity I had to help – or at least to feel like I was helping.

I wanted Nancy to live, was horrified at the thought of her dying before her daughter was in her teens. Much of what I read was dire. The prognosis was poor. Even a cursory glance through non-expert websites made this plain, while expert ones populated with greyscale, lunar-like images of the insides of bodies made positive outcomes frankly unlikely. To Donal, my constant sounding board, I expressed the horror of these realizations: the shocking awareness that all lives could unravel at any time. I was devastated, so how must Nancy and her family feel? It was too terrible to contemplate. To Nancy and to her husband, I focused on the upsides: that she'd responded well to chemo, had, a few months after my mother died, come through major surgery well. Like the untrained medical reader I was, I sought out studies that showed remission, cure, and found enough of them to encourage me to encourage her.

To try to combat the ever-present nausea, she tried many things. Cannabidiol oil, sold everywhere in Ireland by that time as CBD, proved useless. Friends stealthily sent jelly sweets with THC that were legal to buy in several American states but unavailable in Ireland. These plastic packages of gummy bears were among the most highly prized items in the house now, with Nancy figuring how many she could take per day or week to make them last through her chemo. At one time a keen user of pot, Nancy then found out that she could request permission to access medical marijuana. The paperwork for this process was arduous, involving requests to various hospital people as well as requiring her family doctor to complete forms. But eventually, she became among the first people in Ireland to be granted a licence for medicinal marijuana.

She was too ill to go herself, of course, so her husband set off one day for a particular dispensary in the Netherlands. I sat with her while he travelled. On their family phones – hers, her husband's, her daughter's – was a group tracking app so that they could see each other's locations. This was something of a preoccupation with Nancy through the years, and that day stays in memory as strange and out of time as she kept her eyes on his progress. He was off the plane and in the airport. He was passing through the airport into the train station. Now he should be on the train and then, yes, the dot was moving again. It was almost as if he was on a sting operation and we were carefully monitoring his movements to know that he was safe.

After he had collected the package with its paperwork, their daughter arrived home from school and I left Nancy and she alone together as Nancy's husband made the return journey by train, plane and car. The challenges of the day – the exhausting fact of travelling overseas merely to collect an item from a chemist – remain in my mind, since they indicate not only the lengths to which we go for our loved ones, but also the strange reassurance in being able to know where your beloved is, to see them moving and alive: a real-time version of the mind's eye. His moving dot gave her such comfort – it was not merely the fact of what he was collecting but her anxiety for *him* to be okay, to be getting about alright on his own. This vigil was a way of being with him, of showing how much she loved and appreciated him.

One thing that Nancy and I shared was a nervousness about flying. We exchanged tips and, when I told her about an expert's suggestion of asking a friend to track your flight as a way of reminding yourself that what you were doing was absolutely normal and safe, she immediately volunteered to be my tracker, as she put it. This was after her diagnosis, during an upswing. I was preparing, mentally, for a long trip, from Dublin to Hong Kong and on to Sydney and later to New Zealand. It had been several years since Donal and I had travelled that distance; I hadn't wanted to go too far from my mom. But after she died I was invited to something in Sydney and we jumped at the chance, delighted to be able to take the boys to Australia and to visit family in New Zealand again. But I was anxious; it had been ages since I'd been on long-distance flights. Nancy was endlessly encouraging, reminding me how much the kids would get out of the trip. You got this, she said.

I was the moving dot on her screen, and I knew this as I semi-slept in the body of the plane as it flew endlessly over Europe and Russia and then China. When we landed in Hong Kong and I turned on my phone there was an immediate message to say she'd seen I'd landed, that she'd track the next flight too.

Nancy's phone was never far from her and was permanently charging so that she could keep in touch with her huge number of friends. After she died, I sometimes opened our chat on my screen, scanning through the thousands of messages, sometimes looking just at the last ones as if I could learn something new from them: as if I could have written different things and the ending of the story could have been changed. The flashing cursor at end of our exchanges was like the tickets I kept for the TGV after my father died: the flashing suggested I could start the conversation again, that another future was possible.

The moving dot that tracked Nancy's own being and said all was okay disappeared when she died. While her digital afterlife persisted through various online platforms, the live dot – that was gone. I cherished the messages, the record of them. In the lockdown months following her death, when it seemed that not just Nancy but the entire world had disappeared, I opened them sometimes to see that yes, she had been here, she had been real, and was comforted by the fact of her having existed. Afterwards I would text her husband, sister, mother, saying nothing in particular because what was there to say? What language could be useful? What comfort could I possibly offer in the face of their tremendous loss?

Thinking of you, I often wrote. *Hope you are doing okay*.

One day not too long after she'd died I opened the messages and, before my eyes, the entire archive disappeared. It had not occurred to me that if Nancy's phone was wiped, as it evidently had been, this would happen. I grieved again, staring at the empty chat. I kept her number in my 'favourites', where it remains, with the tiny star by her name.

*

The weed helped. The nausea lessened. As time went on, there were further positives. Chemo was through, the surgery gotten over, blood markers stabilized. It is easy to write that sentence, all too easy to summarize a number of agonizing months; it seems almost wrong that the experience can be so briefly described – that words skim over pain and panic attacks and such sickness. But while during those months it had seemed as though life would never again be easy or joyous, the time was endured as time must be.

Gradually, Nancy's hair began to grow, her head to clear, days began to seem slightly – ever so slightly – less medicalized. She planned a family trip to Amsterdam, her favourite place. We were often able to meet her aim of a kilometre a day walk, slowly making our way down the path and back. If Ruth Bader Ginsberg is doing 10,000 steps and yoga, I gotta get my target, she'd say. Some days she was well enough that we drove from her house to the coast. Her legs weren't up to going down the steep slope to her favourite sea-glass cove, but we sat at a bench above it and gazed out to sea, her head scarf sometimes coming loose in the persistent breeze. She took no-filter photos for Insta and Facebook, rested for the walk back to the car. She resumed making art, began jamming with friends again on a weekly basis as the summer rolled on.

One day she called me to say that she was at the top of the sea-glass beach, having gone down and managed the steps back up, but was exhausted now: could I come and meet her and bring water? I headed over quickly; she was thirsty and so proud of her achievement – and we sat there happily, looking past the cannons and the jagged remains of Black Castle. The cancer was gone. The doctors said that things looked good.

In those months Nancy asked regularly about my mom, though I spoke of my grief with reluctance. I did not want to burden Nancy with more thinking about death, about its aftermath. We focused on her progress, on summer plans, marking small milestones. When she and her husband and child made the autumn trip to Amsterdam we all hoped that the worst was behind her. In a nod to Nancy's musical career, they'd decided to stay in the same hotel in which John Lennon and Yoko Ono had been photographed in bed. They'd gotten poffertjes, eaten stroopwafels. She'd done it, had a family holiday that compensated for hospital time, all of the time away from her beloved child.

Her elation after the trip was matched, though, by a profound exhaustion. It had been so much harder than she'd anticipated, walking short distances around the city. But she geared up for the holiday season, making artwork, preparing to release a single that had come out of the summer jams, spending hours listening to newer and better versions of the track. Its release was such an achievement – would have been for anyone at any time – but under the circumstances, following what she had thought was the loss of her voice during treatment, it was a triumph.

When her cancer returned I was out of the country, having taken those flights that she tracked for me. This time I was on my phone, sitting on the deck of an idyllic house in the North Island of New Zealand. In the corner of the garden was a peach tree. It was early in the season and the peaches were miniatures of themselves, tight with fur. Donal and the kids and I were playing cards in the shade, saying how miraculous it was to have such fruit growing in your garden. We were looking forward to Donal's sister and husband arriving. The air was warm and we were beginning to think about dinner, fish and chips. I loved the evening stroll down to collect it, pictures of Santa on a surfboard hanging from every lamp post, the town still quiet in the weeks before Christmas, the song of the sea everywhere; our feet perpetually sandy.

Nancy's call came in that space and her distress was deeply shocking against the backdrop. The cancer had returned. Further surgery wasn't an option, so she would undergo more chemo. The incongruity of my surroundings with Nancy's condition was, of course, the incongruity between life and death, recalling for me the moments in the phone booth when I'd heard about my dad: the way that everything continued to whirl on, the relentlessness rubbing up against the reassurance of it. I was so far away. Even more so than at home, I could do nothing, and her loss was prefigured and loomed over me, so that I felt again the strangeness of beginning to wade through the sticking fields of grief while a loved one was still alive. And my sorrow, while profound, was still only that of a friend. My insides clutched at themselves thinking of her family.

Will I fly back? I asked her.

There's nothing, she sobbed, there's nothing you can do. Stay there for now. And I'll track you home.

*

For several weeks afterwards before our return home to Ireland, Donal and I went for early-morning runs together. We ran through landscapes strewn with great boulders thrown by exploding volcanoes of the past. The rock configurations – everywhere – served as a reminder of life's randomness. As we ran and, later in the day, as we drove past more of those rocks here and there – Christmas shopping, meeting nieces and nephews, visiting museums – I would feel the terror of Nancy's illness sweep over me again.

*

A sign that Nancy felt particularly unwell was that she said she wanted me to come in to the hospital. She'd made it through Hanukkah and Christmas at home, despite noting that the cancer juice seemed to be filling her body again. Through the previous year she had returned at different times to hospital to have the fluid drained, spending a night or two there, and she texted morose updates on the litres that were spilling away from her. Where once the record had been a litre and a half, it now tipped in at five. She couldn't stop comparing these amounts to soft-drink bottles. Five litres of Coke, that's how much they've tapped me for now. Sometimes there would be an accompanying picture to show the strange colour of the liquid. Breathing was extremely uncomfortable with so much fluid rushing to refill any space around her organs, and she now relied on the oxygen tank all the time. Her beloved sister flew over from the States for a few days. I hadn't wanted to intrude on their time, stopping by only to drop off food – a tin of her favourite walnut butter cookies (called Mexican wedding cakes in my house and Russian tea balls in hers) – and have a doorstep chat, a dread mounting in my mind. As soon as Nancy's sister returned home, as soon as the holidays were officially over, the energy slid out of her.

Nancy had specific traditions that she liked to enact on New Year's Eve: a countdown TV show with her husband and daughter, particular foods, and the going through of a memory jar. During the year she'd jot down on small pieces of paper special days or moments and place them in the jar; on New Year's Eve, they opened them. I don't remember if they did that that New Year's. Even Nancy's determined gratitude would have struggled to add to the jar in recent months. By then the rule of our conversations had been that I would not ask how she was feeling, because it was always the same: awful.

By New Year's Day she was texting to say that they were going to the hospital. She had to get drained again, she thought. Maybe she needed another blood transfusion. Procedures that had once seemed terrifying were now routine, and she prepared to go in with a degree of confidence that a four- or five-day stay would see her readying herself for the drive back home. When her husband had to return to work and would be busy for several days, I asked if she'd like me to come in. But when she said yes, I took that as a sign that, like me, she observed a certain trajectory. There were only small fractions of time during which she felt relief, and the time between trips to hospital for worsening symptoms was diminishing.

EULOGY

Perhaps in common with others of you, Nancy was my friend despite the fact that I know hardly anything about David Bowie. By the time that David Bowie died in 2016, however, I did know enough about Nancy to call her on that January day. Given that this awful event has had to take place, there is a tiny comfort in the fact that today happens to be David Bowie's anniversary. I like to think that it might get a Nancy nod.

In speaking today, I am conscious of trying to do justice to someone to whom it would be impossible to do justice to in any brief time; I am also conscious that I am speaking as but one representative of literally hundreds upon hundreds of friends and relatives who are grieving for Nancy. All of us here, in addition to so many who cannot be here in this room, have stories, favourite moments, and I hope that F and H especially will get to hear all of those in the months and years to come.

I think it's worth telling you how I met Nancy, because just as I suspect Nancy tolerated others like me who weren't Bowie superfans, I suspect that many of us have similar stories. I met Nancy quite randomly, at a meeting to try to generate interest in a new Educate Together second-level school for North Wicklow. H was 4, as was my son C, and my 'little O', as Nancy persisted in calling him until even last week, was indeed a little baby in a sling. We talked, discovered that we were both Americans in Wicklow, exchanged phone numbers, and became friends, going on road trips with the kids, making pilgrimages into Dublin to museums, hanging on the beach, going for walks. Nancy really did make friends like that: instantaneously, everywhere. At those kinds of meetings. At craft circles. At art classes. In songwriting workshops. At gigs. In college, in coffee shops. In her estate, and all over the world when she traveled – last summer in Glendalough we ran into the family she stayed with on her first trip to Ireland, and last week she showed me pictures someone had just sent her on Facebook from a long-ago trip to Israel. In fact, it could be a kind of party game: where did Nancy not make friends? (The school, by the way, now H's, did happen, in no small part because Nancy was relentless in collecting expressions of interest: I'd like to have seen any of you try to turn her down outside the local supermarket!)

While I didn't know Nancy as a child or a teenager, one of my favourite stories that she told me was of how she embarked on an early sold-out tour – I think perhaps she was 13 or 14? – of local nursing homes and a home for handicapped children, Sea Shore Gardens, to which she enterprisingly offered her services as a ventriloquist act with her dummy Arty and booked herself gigs. Can you imagine the joy in a nursing home of watching a teenage Nancy getting to have Arty say all the bad words?! That image, of this beautiful, hilarious, vivacious girl telling jokes and singing for me sums up so many elements of Nancy's personality: enterprising, determined, willing to put in the hard graft of hours – in this case of practice in front of different crowds – and also superbly generous in a surprising, unusual way, bringing pleasure to people who were challenged by disability, age, loneliness.

Those early gigs, of course, led to an exciting career. Born in Margate, New Jersey, Nancy attended university in Philadelphia and there established herself in the music scene. A gifted and prolific singer-songwriter, Nancy performed at countless venues around the city, supporting and encouraging musicians and making loyal friends and fans. In 1998, she won a talent contest to perform at Lilith Fair, a major concert tour founded by Sarah McLachlan, one of my then-favourite singers ('she was pretty good', Nancy said to me when I expressed excitement, in a tone that said 'but was not David Bowie'). She also appeared as a guest vocalist with the jam band Moe, unforgettably singing 'Great Gig in the Sky'.

Many of us here in Ireland did not know Nancy in her US singing days but were still lucky enough to hear her sing, whether on stage or in the car, and I'm sure many of you also share with me a memory of hearing her voice for the first time and just being awestruck. In Ireland she continued to write and produce music, releasing *Under the Stars* with Fran King in 2008; her last single, 'Accommodation Road', was recorded and released only last year with a group of musicians she absolutely loved to jam with.

But of course it wasn't just music for which Nancy had a talent. She was, altogether, one of the most artistic people I've ever known. Sitting down to have a cuppa (though of course Nancy never, ever had tea or coffee)? Nancy was embroidering something, perfecting French knots, and in all likeliness for a gift. Walking the dogs? Nancy was collecting sea glass: 'that is a perfect bird', she would say. 'Look at that for an amazing heart'. Her embroidery, her sewing, her watercolours, her sea glass art (and jewelry), her albums all spoke of a phenomenally talented woman. While I particularly cherish a piece of embroidery that she gave me after my mother died – at a time when she was already seriously ill herself – I think that my favourite of Nancy's artistic undertakings – and which again speaks volumes about her – was the fact that she sewed – and made into 3D soft toys – drawings that H did when she was little. She was, to use a Nancyism, the mommyest.

Nancy was never only about herself. She championed so many things and people. Artists all over Ireland, whose work she not just displayed so beautifully in her home but also spoke about and tagged on social media, benefitted from her commitment to and love of art. One of the highlights of her year was the craft fair at the RDS and she was thrilled to be invited to present and sell her beautiful pieces there in 2018, despite the agonizing amount of work that it took, again at a time that she was feeling terribly unwell. Nancy also championed local businesses and countless charities and contributed generously to so many that eventually she set up the first '100 Women' chapter in Ireland not long before her diagnosis, as usual a magnet and bringer-together of people.

Nancy had a hundred interests, an opinion on everything. She loved Ireland; she loved Irish sheep. She was thrilled to support the Together for Yes campaign here in Ireland, and devastated when Trump was elected. When I called her that morning on the way to work I think it was the only time we didn't actually talk at all, just cried and used even more curse words than usual for a Philly girl and a New Yorker. She was knowledgeable about loads of things and also showed interest in everything you were doing too. Once my children started rock climbing competitively, articles and links to films would arrive by text and email (along with a regular reminder that it was a crazy sport). Every 16 June I would get a text: Happy Bloomsday from your only Jewish friend in Ireland, she wrote one year. She remembered people's birthdays, wrote thank you cards, was anxious to return Tupperware, dishes, a carrier bag. All of these tiny acts, these tiny elements, contributed to make Nancy the generous, supportive, and extraordinarily loving person that she will always be.

It is impossible to talk about Nancy, though, without talking about her family and her overwhelming love for them, and most especially for F and H, her 'rock' and her 'best girl'. Last Thursday and Friday, I was most privileged to be able to sit with Nancy in the hospital and talk with her. Our talk was typically Nancy, and also representative of that tremendous love of hers for these two amazing people. After we agreed for the hundredth time that Joey from *Friends* was indeed the best, Nancy spoke again of H's birth, telling me not only about the traumatizing ordeal of having to tolerate someone in the hospital touching her towels (!), but of the overwhelming sense of joy that this perfect little girl was indeed hers, and was going home with her and F. She talked about F and her good fortune in meeting and marrying him. We also spoke again of how, when H was little, Nancy used to ask her not to repeat ABCs or point to a horse or cat on the page of a picture book but to identify which of the Beatles was singing on any given track. We watched a few of H's brilliant and hilarious short films, of which Nancy was endlessly proud. At one point she lay back, closed her eyes, smiled and said simply, 'I love them'. The look of joy and contentment on her face at that moment brought tears to my eyes.

There was one area that Nancy did not excel – and since Nancy was so honest I'm going to have to be, too – and that was … cooking. Nancy widely praised dishes that she loved. So while I may not have met all of you, I know about your pickles, your dahl, your cinnamon buns. It was not in her *praise* of food that Nancy was glorious, however: she missed a calling, perhaps, as one of the funniest food critics ever. A bread was not smooshy enough, she would say, or a cake so dry that she wanted to spread butter on it. Woe betide you if you brought her 'slimy' watermelon. The head chef in St Vincent's Private Hospital got a lecture recently about how vegetarians required more than boiled potatoes and vegetables that were smooshy (a favourite food-descriptor word). Really, you'd give this to your kids? she asked him. Thoroughly chastised, they ended up sending someone down the road for a supermarket frozen pizza for her so that she could eat only the melted cheese, and chips from a takeaway on another occasion. This area in which she did not excel, though, was also turned into a creative outlet, a hilarious blog, one of two that she kept, and one of which was nominated for an Irish blogging award. 'It all goes to the same place' served (and I quote) 'as a communal place to commiserate our cooking catastrophes and remember that ItAllGoesToTheSamePlace'. 'Tastes so good, looks so wrong', the tagline went. Rather than describe the blog, I think it's best to let Nancy just speak for herself, from 6 years back, of an attempt to make sushi:

> I cut the cucumbers and carrots thinly, I had my cream cheese ready. My child didn't have enough patience to let the rice cool so we gave it a go. The warm rice, by the way – made the cream cheese melt. That makes the smush even smushier. Was I supposed to do something to the Nori before rolling? Because I didn't! Cutting it was a disaster, as my "good Ikea knife" didn't really cut it.
>
> And the taste, oy vey. How could something that had no fish taste so much like fish? I know this blog

> is supposed to be about "looks bad, tastes good" but…(I just trailed off there.)
>
> I now have even less of a problem paying the big bucks for the professionals to rock my sushi. Good luck with yours.

Nancy kept her sense of humour throughout her illness. She still joked about her hope that one of her songs would get picked up as the theme song for a much talked about but never-yet-appeared Happy Pear TV show. On Friday she told me that one of the nurses asked her why her drink was 'making a noise'. You can imagine how high her eyebrows went. 'Are you effing kidding me?' she said to me. 'Why does no one in this country know about ice?' She was also upbeat to the end, talking about her 50th birthday last Thursday. In between relentless rounds of chemo and surgery and awful side effects she managed to write and record a song, made well over a hundred pieces of art, traveled to her beloved places, the Netherlands and Achill, and, most importantly, got to spend more time with those she loved most. She was so happy to have had her beloved sister over so recently, as well as her parents, her brother and his wife. Many close friends had wanted to visit, but she kept hoping that she would be able to welcome them when well again, ready to hit her favourite Wicklow and Dublin spots, ready to sing.

To F and H, and to all of Nancy's family, I just want to say that all of this love for Nancy is your inheritance, and paltry as it is in comparison to having her with you, we hope that you can take some small comfort in it.

For a long time now, I've been hoping that I would find a red sea glass heart on some beach for Nancy. (I even thought about cheating and buying her one on eBay.) But Nancy herself was that rarest bit of sea glass, the one in a billion. So the next time you are on the beach, take the deepest breath. Look for sea glass. And when you find a piece, any piece at all, think of Nancy: 'Look at that for an amazing heart'.

PRISMS

After Nancy's funeral, Donal drove home with our children; O wasn't feeling well, and we thought it would be better if I wasn't under pressure to leave. Alone, I drove the back road to Nancy's, glad of a few minutes to gather myself before facing people. I let my mind go blank.

I brought biscuits and the makings of sandwiches, hastily preparing them in the galley kitchen alongside two neighbours and friends of Nancy's I'd come to know during her illness. We piled baguettes and sliced pans filled with crumbed ham slices and cheese, the stoic centrepiece of so many wakes and after-funeral gatherings in Ireland. If it had been a get-together at Nancy's while she was alive, I would have baked her sister-in-law's challah for her; Russian tea balls/Mexican wedding cakes; the beet burgers she liked with feta and spring onions; aubergine and lentil moussaka: all things I had regularly made for her. But she was dead and I was not interested in cooking.

Nancy's mother, heartbreakingly mid-flight when her oldest daughter died, had ordered catering platters of cheese, crackers and grapes. When we removed their clear lids the plastic gleamed black and cold beneath the food. There were cakes, too, and I started to make tea. I wondered if anyone had fed the fish, which were in a small tank on the windowsill. There was little counterspace, and it was now covered with boxes of biscuits, cardboard containers with windows of cake, as people arrived.

The food shared space with the signs of Nancy's illness: hard orange plastic bottles of prescription tablets, stacks of pillboxes. The evidence went beyond the kitchen, though. Everywhere you looked there was medical equipment. They'd had the stairlift installed only weeks before and Nancy had cried with the relief of being able to get upstairs to shower rather than face the ordeal of the steps. The wheelchair had yet to be collected by the health service; it leaned against a hall wall, collapsed in bars of shining silver and blue vinyl. The hospital bed had vanished as if with Nancy herself, collected in rapid time by the company we'd called a year and a half earlier. Where the bed had been, the portable oxygen machine and its supplementary canisters of air were pushed together in an awkward huddle. Because the dining table had to be cleared for food, masses of pill bottles, bandages, dressings, spare tubing for the oxygen machine, and other detritus had been piled atop the piano, itself already crammed with photos and artwork. It made my head unsteady, so I stayed by the sink, tasking myself with the responsibility of washing mugs and teacups as Nancy had described doing at her father-in-law's funeral several years earlier.

As I often did, I felt shy, wanting to step back from the busyness of the event, remain in the background. People found me, though. I knew few of Nancy's large circle of friends; our friendship had been independent of other groups, based on that chance meeting about starting up a school. But because I'd spoken at the funeral and was one of the public faces of grief for Nancy, strangers sought me out. Several people jokingly asked if I would speak at their funerals. One man told me that there might be a market in writing eulogies. It was so specific, he told me, what you said. It was really about Nancy. This made me wonder about eulogies themselves, what it was about the experience of grief that can leave us wordless, even blind us to the particularities of the one we mourn.

*

When I was small my mother bought me a triangular prism at the New York Planetarium gift shop. It was always cool, a solid block of glass that fitted into my hand but not naturally; its shape meant that you were always conscious of holding it, of its lines against your skin. I would sit on the blue carpet of my sunny room with the prism in my hands, turning it over, holding it up to the light at different angles, casting rainbows on the white walls. Despite having the science explained to me, I was intrigued with something beyond the explanation, with the idea that you could hold this marvel in your hand, create it again and again for yourself. The prism came back to me when I thought through what I had wanted to do in the eulogies I'd given.

I had sought to see my mother, see Nancy, and in after years my father, through such a prism, trying to hold what I knew and loved of them in my mind, to cast lights and colours from various angles – not just my own. I had sought to show some of their aspects, their individual ordinariness that ran up against the fact of their being, at the same time, extraordinary, absolutely loved. Wasn't that what it was to be human? To be composed of the same deltaic systems of pumping blood and coursing thought – and yet also different to all others, in minute and even in seemingly meaningless ways. But those fractional distinctions, the crazy, chance-driven differences, resulted in people with whom we could fall in love, people with whom we could connect (in the way I longed to connect as a teenager), people without whom we ourselves would not be the same, surely not ourselves.

It was strange to be complimented on the quality of a eulogy. It was not a piece of writing for which I expected praise; in some ways my mind did not grasp a eulogy as a piece of writing at all. It was something else, something to do with the prism and the ways in which if you sat long enough with it in your hand allowing light to surge through it, the strange, surreal beauty of the world possessed you.

Growing up in New York we'd had that pool in our building, a sauna in each changing room. From youngest childhood I'd spent hundreds of hours swimming before surrendering to the dark heat of the sauna, where there was often a friend, a neighbour, someone who wanted to talk – or not: perhaps I might meet someone who, like me, was content to lie there in silence, hearing only the hot ache of the wood. What struck me, through the years, was the fact that every person I met in that sauna was beautiful. The miracle of the body – its unending variation, its power to simultaneously make us all the same – was remarkable to me. Sitting there, talking with various people about their lives, about the weather, I was regularly profoundly moved, and as moved by those sitting or lying in the dark quiet without speaking, in their bodies that contained all of their life experience. At a young age I began to wonder whether if you subjected any individual to enough focus, enough attention, there was an exceptional, extravagant beauty in them that would be found nowhere else.

Some people broke down after Nancy's funeral; they wept in my arms in the kitchen, in the hallway. One woman told me that Nancy had years before given her a substantial amount of money to enable her and her then small children to leave an abusive relationship. This woman Nancy had never mentioned was overcome by the loss of a person who had changed her life, someone she'd lost contact with. There was guilt, shame, longing in her grief. Why hadn't Nancy told her she was ill? She could have repaid her in some way. Brought food. Sat with her. Run her to hospital appointments. I recognized that this woman needed something from me in the way that my dying loved ones had. I reassured her. I told her I knew that Nancy would not have expected anything in return.

That Nancy would have been simply happy knowing that her life had turned around. As she cried into my neck, a pair of tall teenagers loomed behind her in the hall, the seriousness of their beautiful young faces a clear reminder of what Nancy's gift had achieved.

Another woman was a neighbour who had begun walking the dogs when Nancy went into hospital. These dogs danced in place when this neighbour was near; she was the outside world of smells and adventure, attention, love, the holder of the leash and the one to let them free. Her sense of loss concerned me because it was not only the loss of her friend, but also her routines. I recognized this, having gone through it with my mother and knowing that I would go through it again now. For weeks after my mother died I had to remind myself not to drive to the nursing home; several times I turned automatically down the side road that headed that way. I'd go to buy flowers for her and realize she was gone. I no longer saw the other residents of the nursing home, either: they became unfinished books that I worried about. For this woman it would be similar, the revision of her life patterns. Nancy was dead, and so this neighbour's routines would need to change. Nancy's husband and child could walk the dogs now. This woman's sense of self was deeply rooted in her helpfulness, her dedication to her friend's family. So much so that, as she cried and we hugged I suspected that she would continue to walk the dogs. I see her there in the narrow kitchen, her kind, pretty face flushed with emotion.

After death there is the longing for the lost person. But there is also the loss of self in relation to that person. We can become bewildered. How do we act, when the other player has disappeared?

*

My father and mother died over twenty years apart. Two years after my mother died, Nancy died. These are almost physical landmarks in my life, I was so profoundly changed after each death. With each of these losses, death seemed to move closer. The movement began abstractly, with my father's rapid demise and disappearance; I wasn't aware until after he died that it would impact me at all. My mother's death was the one I feared most, conscious that my emotional reliance on her all through childhood meant that I could, possibly, fall apart once she was gone. That I did not is more a testament to her than to me. I had young children when my mother died, and her death felt close, though not threatening.

Nancy's death had a different taste to it: someone so near to me in age, someone I spoke to daily, someone with whom a decade of friendship had entwined me in ways I didn't fathom until she was ill. Mutual friends and acquaintances felt their lives filling with fear. No one said it, but you could see in everyone's eyes real relief that, if such awful things happened, they happened to someone else. It was the same fear that I saw in people's faces when I spoke of losing the baby; it was a worry that loss, illness, death – all were contagious. The fear, the fear not just for Nancy for but the self, spurred acts of extraordinary generosity that made me think that even humans who didn't believe acted with religious intent and fervour when faced with the insurmountable. Meals appeared on the doorstep as practical assistance, but also to appease the gods, it seemed to me. And everyone – myself included – sought explanations, wanted reasons. Just as I had when my father had been diagnosed with cancer decades earlier, Nancy's family and friends wanted some reassurance that this had happened – cancer had developed – because of something else. That there were genetic factors, unknown. Or that it was related to her youthful smoking. Because it was too near, too terrifying to consider that it was simply random. Bad luck. Tiny movements of tiny cells that set off cataclysms in the life cycle. She was too young; it was not fair. And so instead of smoking incense in temples, instead of fiddling with rosary beads, we cooked, we gave lifts, we sent things that might offer comfort and relief, however momentary. We offered these things in the hope that they spoke love and could make a difference, weave a spell of good luck, encourage cells to heal. We knew – or at least I knew – that the medical treatment was the only real hope, but I wanted more than that: miraculous cure, redemption.

This is so stupid, she said to me on her deathbed. This is so stupid. And I understood because it did feel stupid. Surely it was a mistake; we could rewind.

As a musician and singer who spent endless hours going over tracks, rerecording elements and relaying them, trying to distil a segment of song into perfect form, Nancy understood the power of the do-over. In the studio it was possible to move backwards and forwards with sliders on mixing desks. You could take fragments and reorder time. But on that last hospital bed, no longer with the strength to even slide open her phone, she was, finally, resigned.

This is so stupid.

I did not say this at her funeral. I did not say that I was angry that she was dead. I did not say that I was looking for reasons that this had happened that I could not find, or that I had been grieving for her for months and months. Because none of it was about me, naturally : my grief was a pittance compared to that of her family's. I did not say that speaking was a performance I felt I owed Nancy, who had been a professional performer.

I knew now, all the years after my father's death, that standing up to speak at a funeral was not unlike the anxiety of stepping into the role on a stage. You tried to become a space for other people's memories; you tried to give voice to them. And I was alert to the fact that, unlike my father, my mother and Nancy, I was not a natural performer: I preferred to remain backstage or to sing back-up, do harmonies.

*

When Nancy began using sea glass in her art, I, like other of her friends, began collecting it for her. My youngest son and I often had half an hour before his brother finished school, so we went to the harbour to skim and throw stones, and to walk the short c of the shore with our eyes fastened to the shifting world beneath our feet. We collected handfuls of sea glass – aquamarine teardrops, green triangles, frosted white ovals, occasional nibs of cobalt blue – my little one's fists opening to empty his finds into my hands, which were so boned and veined beside his. When we returned to the car, I emptied my pockets into a small cup for odd coins. If that was full, we'd make do with a plastic bag, and when next I'd see Nancy I'd carry it into her.

She always poured it out and spread it with a deft hand, admiring pieces, remarking on notable ones. All of it went into water for cleaning. Later, though I didn't see her do it, she sorted it by colour and by shape; in her pretty cabin built for art-making were bowls and containers of sea glass, stacks of them, thousands of pieces of bottles and perhaps other objects reduced to pure colour by the sea.

After she died, I still haunted the beach; of course I did, since it was a place Donal and the kids and I went often to swim and kayak and meet friends. Chatting with other parents while our children paddled or pier-jumped or skimmed kayaks along the water, I found my hands trawling through the warm stones, seeking and finding those bits of glass, examining them in my fingers, pocketing those that were best: deconstructed stained-glass windows that I could hold in my hands, inadvertent prisms through which to try to see. But when I spilled them into the cup in my car, there was nowhere to empty them; the cup overflowed and the glass fragments began to fill the small area where I kept sunglasses, chewing gum. I couldn't keep collecting the glass. Instead, I started leaving my finds in neat piles somewhere – on the edge of the pier, on steps where people sat to towel themselves dry after swimming. They seemed so substantial, these mounds of gathered colour: offerings of a kind. I saw a small girl squeal and scoop one up once as we left, delighted with the fact of a hoard that had simply appeared.

When a piece of glass emerges smooth from the sea – its colour dimmed and softened, its edges long gone – it has spent approximately half a century in the water.

This is longer than Nancy lived.

IMAGINED COMFORT

I have a memory of a conversation that did not take place. In it I tell my mom about Nancy's diagnosis, choking back tears. Oh love, my mother says, that is dreadful, dreadful news. She says it in her usual caressing tone. And she says that she wished it were her instead, remarking on the unfairness of a woman not yet fifty being handed such a sentence while she, in her early eighties and miserable in her own diagnosis, only wished to go.

My mother was not coherent or vocal enough to have had this conversation when Nancy was diagnosed. Yet I hear my mother's concern, her attempt to offer comfort her wish that things could be otherwise. I remember this conversation as if it had happened.

HEARTBEAT

In the hospital atrium I am aware that the last time I was here was to see Nancy. I am aware that I am more than a decade older than my grandmother on her death at home in 1938, that I am now older than Nancy was when she died. Even after a few years, there is a startling familiarity to the configuration of tables and chairs clustered near a coffee bar, the blue-outfitted doctors and consultants striding about. I walk upstairs and remember walking down that evening almost three years ago. I'm not going to the same ward, but up only one more flight of stairs is the high-dependency unit with its few patients and extreme levels of medical attention; there are people there now who are in dire straits. It feels surprising that most people are walking and talking normally, as if no one is dying here; but the dying are contained, somewhere behind closed doors or discreet curtains, surrounded with accumulations of medical paraphernalia.

I am checked in first by a nurse who weighs me, and then by a nurse half my age who calls me darling and completes the first of many forms. A third nurse goes through my medical history and instructs me about where to leave my clothes and bag (in a small wardrobe in the corner). There is one of those tables on wheels that can be slid over the bed; on it is a silver pitcher of water and a clean glass with a napkin covering it but I am instructed not to drink anything yet. For yesterday's pelvic scan it was the opposite; I had to arrive with my bladder full to bursting to enable better imaging. Today I am not allowed any liquids or foods, and while I am not yet hungry the water is tempting.

After the first three nurses there are others. There is the Dublin porter who wheels me down to pre-op (I'm uncomfortable about this but am not allowed to walk) alongside another young Irish nurse who tells me about studying at UCD. Then there is a Filipino nurse who describes how much busier it is since Covid but who, despite the increased work load, is still glad the pandemic is over. The South African surgeon pops in and I sign consent forms for her; she is cheerful and brisk. Another male nurse, Irish this time, pushes me into the room that leads towards four theatres, and there I remain for a few minutes on my own, eyeing neat cabinets with labels of unknown instruments and drugs.

The anaesthetist, whose accent I cannot place, comes in to insert a canula into my hand (*deep breath in and you'll feel a scratch*) and then I am left again. It is quiet in the blue and grey and white room with its clean surfaces.

Four pages pinned on a board list the order of surgeries for the four doctors in theatre that morning. My eye scans the small writing and I try to figure out which of the surgeries is mine; the procedures all sound almost the same, so I guess by the time instead. I can hear staff chatting and laughing in one of the theatres, distantly, and I wish I could see them, always curious about experts in their environments.

I watch everything with interest. I am not nervous. A few days earlier I did check with Donal that he knew various passwords for bank accounts, but I have no real alarm. I transfer from the wheeling ward bed to the operating table. When the anaesthetic begins it runs coldly up my arm and I think – ice in my veins. I feel it rise as far as my elbow.

I wake in a recovery room with four beds. The first question the nurse is asking me is about running. I do run, I say, startled at the sudden conversation. How much? she asks. I'm barely awake but thinking: do we have to talk about running right now? The anaesthetist comes over to question me as well. As I try to focus, they point to my heart rate, which is now at a steady 32 bpm. Over the next hour I watch patients come and go from the recovery beds, wheeled in and out by the same porters. The newest nurse talks to me about New York, where her brother lives. She tells me about working on a public ward at the start of the pandemic, how she lived at home at the time and worried constantly about her parents being exposed. She is almost done with her Christmas shopping (it is November) and today is her Friday, she explains, because she has the next three days off. All the while she is observing my heart rate on the screen. I too start to watch it, swivelling round with all of the attachments and tubes to see the green lights, which still hover in the low thirties. While the nurse talks I read the two patients' heart monitors on the other side of the room and see numbers of 59 and 75. When I sit up mine reaches 39.

The anaesthetist isn't in a hurry to let me return to the ward; I am repeatedly asked how much running I do. I think sometimes that I am dreaming: surely the medical staff are not asking me about distance running. Time passes and I continue to watch my heart rate and those of the other patients as they come out of their own surgeries; their heart rates are usually more than double my own. Eventually the anaesthetist and nurse agree that I am okay and, after additional hours back on the ward with the compact wardrobe and the silver jug of water that I am now allowed to pour into the clean glass, I am walking back down the stairs to meet my husband.

I wait in a queue to buy a latte, my legs wobbly, and then walk outside. The autumn sun is already low in the sky and glinting. It is as if I have visited someone, not as if I've had surgery myself; I'm aware that I look like someone casually having a coffee and not a patient who's just alarmed the medical staff. I could have just left my father, my mother, or Nancy on the day she died.

There's a strange gratitude in walking out of hospital on your own feet. In the car beside Donal, cup in one hand, I cling to him with the other, full again of that unspeakable thankfulness.

PRIVATE EULOGY

I sat at Nancy's bedside that penultimate day with dread: my heart raced with fear. As I left the ward, a doctor pulled me aside. Is she aware, he asked, is her family aware of what is happening?

I went home and sat at our kitchen table. I told Donal, deeply unsettled, what I told the doctor: I wasn't sure.

I had always assumed that – from the day of diagnosis – Nancy understood what she was facing. But I had also never felt it my place to ask directly how she felt about this, whether there was anything that she wanted to do to prepare. Those conversations, I felt, were for herself and her family – the awful, life-upending private conversations between loved ones facing permanent parting, preparing for their lives to be rearranged in dramatic fashion, for a child to be motherless.

And yet now I wished I had been braver in my conversations with her. I'd sat by Nancy's bed the whole day with the horrifying worry that she did not seem to know.

Maybe it wasn't, as I thought, that she was keeping the best side out all the time. Maybe it wasn't that she was living under an act-positive-be-positive mantra. The remainder of her life could now be counted off in several dozen hours, yet she exhibited no awareness of this fact. She'd had panic attacks for months and months after her diagnosis; yet now, in the perilous moment, she seemed not to know. What was it about the weight of the illness that made it difficult for her to think clearly? Was it the horror of the situation making avoidance a necessity?

The doctor too was unsettled. I've been very direct, he said. And I knew he had. I'd sat there when he approached the bed that afternoon, his face drawn into a slight frown.

Aww, are you not going to show me your pearly whites? Nancy had demanded. He never cracks a smile, she complained to me in an aside. This was not the surgeon to whom she had presented a needlepointed hoop of ovaries in pink French knots along with a bottle of whiskey, the one who'd told her it was the best present he'd ever received, the first time anyone had embroidered ovaries for him. (No, really? she responded.) This doctor was slightly older, perhaps sixty, a well-known surgeon and researcher who wore expensive casual clothes in camel, beige, cream. He had a young child, Nancy told me, with a new wife.

How're you feeling today, Nancy? he asked her.

I'm hanging in there, she replied. How're you?

I'm grand, Nancy, but I'm really concerned about you.

Really? she said. You gonna get out of here for the weekend and see your kid?

She couldn't accept that this was not a conversation; she wanted to return to a space in which she could talk with everyone, find out their life stories, give them hers.

Now I turned to Donal. Did I have to tell her? Or was that entirely inappropriate? Should I say nothing, watch her run through her remaining hours with that kind of oblivion? But that kind of oblivion might extend to her family, too, who could be shocked beyond measure. I cried knowing that when I went in the next day one of those conversations, the ones I'd assumed were none of my business, far too personal to be, might fall to me.

Can I describe the drive to the hospital that morning, knowing what was ahead? I listened to no music, no radio. The clouds were corrugated and it was not raining but the air was chill. I brought no food, only a photo and some Blu-Tack.

There are talks you never imagine having: asking your friend whether she has thought about dying, soon. I spoke in a roundabout way because I didn't want to ask outright. Hazy with the cumulative toll of her disease and impending unconsciousness, Nancy struggled with my approach, which must have seemed to her strangely philosophical and indirect, as if we were a pair of stoned teenagers imagining what happened after death.

We passed time. I bathed her forehead, her neck, lifting the curls that had begun to grow once more. Eventually I tried again: Nancy, I think your daughter needs to come in.

I don't want her to remember the hospital, she said, her usual refrain. It's so awful in here. Full of sick people.

I was quiet, but then I said, Yes, but I think she needs to come in.

It was the repetition that did it. She opened her eyes to look at me.

You think it's serious.

Yes, I told her.

You think it's that serious, really? You think this is the end? Suddenly she understood: I can still hear the different energy in her voice, an alertness.

I nodded, because words tangled in my throat.

A nurse approached – nurses regularly approached – to check some of the many tubes and elements streaming from Nancy's body.

Do you think I should get my daughter in here? Nancy demanded. Is it serious?

The nurse, one of Nancy's favourites, looked at me and then looked at Nancy and said, If it were me I would want my family around me now.

You think it's the end? Nancy asked us both. Because if it's the end I want my mom here.

Then it would be a good idea to call her, the nurse said. She withdrew with tears in her eyes.

Over the following hour, I dialled Nancy's husband, mother and sister on her phone and handed it over to her, ringing.

For the rest of the day I sat by the bed bathing Nancy's forehead with cold cloths and typing messages to her dearest friends from her phone as she dictated. She was in the same hospital my mother had been in, though my mother had not been in the private section. My mother's

American insurance had not carried over to Ireland, and her ward had often been chaotic. The private wing was calm, highly staffed; Nancy was in high dependency right by the nurse's station. Her bed – elevated, atilt – was far larger than my father or mother's had been since it was connected to machines on all sides. Everything was white and cream metal set against pale grey walls. A window was several feet behind her bed, at almost head height – as if positioned for a visitor who would need to look away, recall momentarily a world beyond the room. I thought of my father's hospital room and its exaggerated New York view, my mother's nursing home room with its drawn curtains and nothing to see. To look away here required getting up, deliberately walking off: something I did each time a nurse or doctor came to examine her, or when Nancy took a short call. There was a golf course below, large trees running in swathes between greens; clusters of people moved here and there but through the glass it wasn't possible to hear the puck of balls arcing into air. Beyond the golf course were houses and small buildings, main roads full of cars heading into town. I could see Sandymount strand, the playground of my mother's childhood, the tide far out.

When Nancy's best friend from college called I went downstairs to get a cup of tea. But I didn't drink it. Instead I watched it smoking on the table in front of me, my eyes unfocused. As I had while my father died, people were eating – muffins and pastries, mostly – while their loved ones recuperated, or underwent surgery, or died. Life demanded sustenance even in extremis. Doctors and interns and nurses in colour-coded scrubs sat in groups among us, not anxious like visitors but glazed with tiredness. There were also patients with family members, those recovering enough to take the glassy elevators down to this interim space between the hospital and the world beyond it. I'd sat here in the recuperative zone with my mother and the children countless times only two years before, the children delighted at the prospect of splitting a chocolate muffin, my mother and I working hard to believe, like them, that we were in a regular café. Watching the tea, I thought of my mother and husband and the children, and then, when enough time passed that Nancy's phone call was likely to have ended, carefully poured the contents of the cup into the bin.

In the lift you could watch the café people recede until they were mere pattern around circular tables. You could exit and walk back into the high-dependency wards as if you could continue to do this day after day and get used to it: create a vision of a tolerable life in which the patients were not trapped in misery but could recover; in which you drank smoking tea.

When I walked back into the unit I could see that Nancy was sleeping, so I paused before the large stand that held her chart. I'd gotten good at understanding notations on Nancy's medical files in only two days, skilled at speed-googling for information and clarification. I read swiftly at the phonebook-thick pile. The newest entry was from that morning; I learned that the walls of her cells were breaking down. This explained why they were discouraging her from drinking: the membranes were becoming so porous that the liquids were able to pass through them. I pictured this and what it might mean, her body flooding. But she was plagued with an irrepressible thirst. She stirred then and asked me to see if they would allow her some iced water.

I pleaded with the nurse for a few sips and, after looking through the chart again herself, standing near enough to me that I could hear her quickening breath, the nurse agreed. She'll need to sit up further, she warned.

I held the straw to her lips. Afterwards Nancy said, This is so stupid. It's so stupid to be dying like this. Am I really dying?

I can't write all of what we talked about. It was a private eulogy, much more important than the other kind. As I spoke to her – she was increasingly too exhausted to talk except in short breathy phrases – I recognized in retrospect that I had done the same for my father. I may not have given him a public eulogy, but I sat by his bed as he lay dying and I told him that I loved him. I told him that I was right there, that I was staying with him. And in the hospital where my mother had begun a slow dissolution away from herself I sat with Nancy and I told her that she had been a great mom, a wonderful partner and friend, that she was loved. I said that I would stay with her as long as she wanted me to. I sang to her, though she was a singer and I am not, because she wondered about the tune of a particular song. It was from a Jewish medley of songs I'd sung with a choral group in New York as a child, and while my voice felt ragged and wispy, I sang it anyway, and she smiled.

I had brought a photo of Nancy's daughter from several years before from our time down the west together, when she'd been in Achill and we'd been across the bay. The photo was of her beautiful child knee-high in the Atlantic off Keem Beach, laughing as a wave splashed around her in iridescent foam. It had been a perfect day: hot, sunny, without cloud. I'd Blu-Tacked the photo to the machine nearest to Nancy, at her eyeline. Look at her, she kept saying. Look at her.

But she couldn't keep her eyes open. The lids were heavy, heavy; they wanted to fall. So I trusted that she had the image of her daughter in her mind and told her about the day of the photo the way that you tell a child a story about themselves when they were small. It was so hot, I told her. Our picnic was crunchy with sand. You had watermelon in a Tupperware container, and grapes. The kids lay on boogie boards, and we pulled them, running in the shallows: their faces alight with the thrill of the cool water and the speed and the glittering day. They scrambled through rock pools, pawed long channels to divert the tide around sandcastles, protested when we smeared ever more sun cream onto their shoulders, noses, cheekbones, the dips at their spines. Everyone's skin was tight and hot at the day's end when we drove in caravan back along the cliffs. We ate at a roadside chipper at tables covered in plastic cloth, and all of us were shining with the crystalline day as if it was something we'd caught, a bubble on the palm. They were so beautiful, our small, wild children, and Nancy had been such a loving, devoted mother to her girl, and H would remember that.

Tell me, she said.

I told her the story of the cove where she found marbles, I told her the story of the cove where she found pottery. I talked about the waves, the sculpted rocks that ran in arms to meet them; the time she had passed roaming that beach with her dogs, the days when a gleam of glass sang out from among shell and stone and leapt into her hand.

In my music app I found a song Nancy had written for her daughter and played it for her and she lay there, quietly.

Maybe I was always supposed to be this old
I'll forever have your hand in mine to walk across the road.

This is so stupid, she repeated then. Can you text again, and see if he's bringing H in? Where is my mom?

I texted.

Your mom is in the air, I told her, and he's bringing H in.

IN THIS HOUSE TOGETHER

There are vanishings.

Games passed on to other children; puzzles made to ensure that they are complete and then donated to a charity shop. The smallest things – the marbles, the tiny dolls, the markers, the cars – are no longer under foot. Lego sets disappear into wardrobes, picture books are consigned to the bottom-most shelves of book cases and thick novels appear instead, stacked by beds and on the coffee table. Instead of paint and glue guns and slime, homework folders, headphones, phones proliferate on the kitchen table. We do not stoop to retrieve object after object; they have disappeared.

It is a sudden scene change; a swipe into teenage years. A swipe from the time that I was a child in New York; a fast-forward from when my father, mother and Nancy were here. A timelapse: the children's sudden appearance in our lives, the accumulations of their things, populating this house that Donal and I built. And now their possessions diminish again as if they are already unconsciously removing themselves – and we confront the realization that these beloved people won't necessarily live with us for many more years.

I think of my parents delivering me in taxis to LaGuardia and Kennedy and Newark airports, waving me through security as I flew back and forth to college and then farther and farther afield; I once rang my mother from a payphone outside Sydney Opera House so that she could share my excitement about seeing *La Traviata* there. Aged twenty I never saw what bravery it took to hold someone and then wave them off, smiling through tears. C and O travel without Donal and I, their own futures tangible now. And I feel grateful that there is still some time here in this house together before the next phase begins.

We listen to them talk together, their lives becoming more and more their own.

ACKNOWLEDGEMENTS

I am grateful to all at The Lilliput Press, and particularly to Seán Farrell for his brilliant insights and advice. Warm thanks as well to my agent, Brian Langan; to Words Ireland for a National Mentorship Award that allowed me to work on this book; to Joanna Walsh for support and encouragement over a crucial period; to Sean Ryder for generous and kind mentorship under the Aurora initiative; to Listowel Writers' Week and Noelle Campbell-Sharpe for a residency at Cill Rialaig Arts Centre; to all at the Tyrone Guthrie Centre at Annaghmakerrig for the space and time to write; to the editors of *Banshee* for publishing an early section of this book as 'Fragments on Houses'; to Djinn von Noorden and to Elske Rahill, both of whom read this text with great care and provided crucial feedback. Thank you as well to my colleagues and friends in the Department of English at Maynooth University; and to Francesca Bratton, Michèle Forbes,

Aoife Glavin (the other of Nancy's 'mountain girls'), Paul Lynch, Christodoulos Makris, Belinda McKeon, Eoin McNamee, Katherine O'Callaghan, Bob Quinn, Fíona Scarlett, and Catherine Talbot for writing conversation and the encouragement to keep going at different times.

I am particularly indebted to Kevin Solon, Pauline Solon, and the late Pedro Hinckeldeyn for access to a space that has been incredibly important to this book and also to our family thank you so much for sharing it with us and for creating such a beautiful atmosphere.

As I wrote this book I was regularly reminded of my good fortune in growing up in a close and supportive community some of whom make appearances here. Warm thanks and love to Betty White, the late Chuck White, Joann Lee and the late Cleta Kensler Holland for their constant kindness and example of what it meant to be good neighbours; and to all of my Waterside girls, who may be glad this is not a book about our teenaged years!

I am grateful to Frankie McBride, Ellen Falkow Auer, Marilyn and Bernie Falkow and to H for being open to my writing in memory of Nancy: when Nancy asked me who would speak for her at her funeral and I said that I would, I never imagined writing a book, but I hope that I have done some aspects of her justice. Nancy Falkow's beautiful music is on Spotify.

'Birth Stories' is in memory of Jamie Scott, Florence Scott, and Gabríel Jónsson.

I am so lucky to be part of a wonderful extended family that has always been an immense support: particular thanks to Paul for many bailouts, only one instance of which appears in this book, and in memory of Tony and Helen, whom we all miss terribly. Thanks most of all to my husband, Donal, and to C and O, all three the loves of my life.

Finally, it is worth saying that while this book is a work of non-fiction, it is a representation of the work of memory. It was not my aim to be accurate about timeframes or the unfolding of events but, instead, to attempt to access the emotional remains of those things. In that sense, elements of this work might be considered fiction.